Ride Out the Wilderness

Melvin Dixon

Ride Out
the Wilderness

*Geography and Identity
in Afro-American Literature*

UNIVERSITY OF ILLINOIS PRESS
Urbana and Chicago

© 1987 by the Board of Trustees of the University of Illinois
Manufactured in the United States of America
C 5 4 3 2 1

This book is printed on acid-free paper.

Library of Congress Cataloging-in-Publication Data

Dixon, Melvin, 1950–   .
  Ride out the wilderness

  Bibliography: p.
  Includes index.
  Partial contents: Go in the wilderness. We'll stand
the storm : slave songs and narratives—down in the
lonesome valley. Wake the nation's underground : Jean
Toomer and Claude McKay.   [etc.]
    1. American literature—Afro-American authors—
History and criticism.   2. Afro-Americans in literature.
3. Landscape in literature.   4. Identity (psychology) in
literature.   I. Title.
PS 153.N5D58   1987   810'.9'896   86-30918
ISBN 0-252-01414-6 (alk. paper)

for
Marcellus Blount
these horizons and beyond

I got a home in that rock, don't you see?
— Traditional

It was a very dangerous thing to let a Negro know navigation.
— Olaudah Equiano

If you only knew the dark Egypt we have come through.
— Ambrose Headen

It is not on any map; true places never are.
— Herman Melville

And if we keep
Our love for this American earth, black fathers,
O black mothers, believing that its fields
Will bear for us at length a harvesting
Of sun, it is because your spirits walk
Beside us as we plough; it is because
This land has grown from your great, deathless hearts.
— Robert Hayden

But the conquest of the physical world is not man's only duty.
He is enjoined to conquer the great wilderness of himself.
— James Baldwin

Contents

Preface

This book examines the relation between geography and identity in selected major works of Afro-American literature. It analyzes images of physical and spiritual landscapes that reveal over time a changing topography in black American quests for selfhood, from early slave songs and narratives, which first located alternative places of refuge and regeneration, to works by modern authors, which construct equally complex geographical figures leading to the discovery and the performance of identity. Images of land and the conquest of identity serve as both a cultural matrix among various texts and a distinguishing feature of Afro-American literary history.

Chapter 1 enlarges and revises an earlier essay of mine that appears in *The Slave's Narrative,* edited by Henry Louis Gates, Jr., and Charles T. Davis (Oxford University Press, 1985). Chapter 4 contains a revision of my essay published in *Black Women Writers,* edited by Mari Evans (Doubleday, 1984). I thank the editors for permission to reprint those essays. I also thank Mrs. Ellen Wright for permission to quote from an unpublished essay by Richard Wright.

I am grateful to the Ford Foundation and the National Research Council and to Queens College for providing fellowship support during the research and writing of this book. Joseph T. Skerrett, Jr., Robert Hemenway, and Michel and Genevieve Fabre encouraged me from the beginning of the project. John Blassingame made facilities at Yale University available during my fellowship tenure there. Robert Stepto, Kimberly Benston, Marcellus Blount, and Bruce Adams read portions of the manuscript and offered useful criticism. Andrew Nargolwala was a tremendous help as my research assistant. Whatever lapses of insight that remain are my own.

Very special thanks go to Richard A. Horovitz, whose sustaining friendship helped to coax this book into being.

Introduction

The night before he was assassinated on April 4, 1968, and scores of angry mourners rioted in cities across the United States, Martin Luther King, Jr., delivered a speech that would become his eulogy. "I don't know what will happen now," he told the rally of marchers at Mason Temple in Memphis, "but it really doesn't matter with me now. Because I've been to the mountaintop. . . . Like anybody, I would like to live a long life. Longevity has its place. But I'm not concerned about that now. I just want to do God's will." As voices in the assembly shouted, "Amen," King continued: "And He's allowed me to go up to the mountain. And I've looked over, and I've seen the promised land" (Lewis, 387). The shouting and cries resounding through the hall bore witness to the widely held dream in King's message. The image of the mountaintop evoked not only the promise but also the performance of freedom.

Through the act and eloquence of his testimony, King must have jolted his listeners backward and forward in time: to the past of slavery and fugitive journeys to free territory, to the present struggle for civil liberties, and to a future of personal and group salvation. Underlying this movement through history is a religious and secular imagery revealing a moral geography of social and political progress. Recurring images of place and person in black popular religious culture, but also in Afro-American literary tradition, stake claims to a physical and spiritual home in America. King's speech, drawn from biblical imagery and the cadence of Negro spirituals, suggested that the need for freedom, felt so acutely during slavery, had resurfaced with equal, if not greater, urgency in the sixties. The freedom songs chanted by marchers, protesters, and sit-in participants were often new musical arrangements of early slave songs. If the dominant society persists in making black Americans feel, as one song puts it, "this world is not my home," and if, as Charles Gordone announced in the title of his contemporary award-winning play, this country offers *No Place to be Somebody,* then black writers, preachers, and political spokespersons as well as the anonymous originators of the songs would seek self-fulfillment in the landscapes they create. Geography and identity link as closely as Ralph Ellison once suggested: "If we don't know *where* we are, we have little chance of knowing *who* we are, that if we confuse the *time,* we confuse the *place;* and that when we confuse these we endanger our humanity, both physically and morally" (*Shadow and Act,* 74). Yet earlier than even Ellison had realized, many singers, poets, and preachers had wielded a verbal compass to discover where and who they were.

In the present study I examine the ways in which Afro-American writers, often considered homeless, alienated from mainstream culture, and segregated in negative environments, have used language to create alternative landscapes where black culture and identity can flourish apart from any marginal, prescribed "place." King's mountaintop is but a culminating image of a triumph of space, of a height of consciousness; the mountaintop has emerged over time from other figures of land and identity that continue to shape the verbal art of black Americans.

Since the major geographical dislocation of blacks from slave-trading Africa and through the nineteenth century, issues of home, self, and shelter have loomed paramount in the black imagination. The physical geography of Afro-American history moves from Africa to the New World, and from the American South to the North (and sometimes back again). The metaphorical geography of Afro-American expression takes a different turn, altering the conventional images of place that link black environments with low social status and spiritual despair. James Baldwin, in *Nobody Knows My Name,* speaks more for the dominant society than for blacks when he writes: "The Negro tells us where the bottom is: *because he is there,* and *where* he is, beneath us, we know where the limits are and how far we must not fall. We must not fall beneath him" (133). Black survival, however, requires that those received values and cultural assumptions associating certain places with low and high social status, or with moral degradation and elevation, be changed. Afro-American literature is replete with speech acts and spatial images that invert these assumptions about place and endow language with the power to reinvent geography and identity.

Through an examination of several key texts, I aim to show how images of journeys, conquered spaces, imagined havens, and places of refuge have produced not only a deliverance from slavery to freedom, but, more important,

2

a transformation from rootlessness to rootedness for both author and protagonist. The novels, narratives, and songs under discussion reveal significant variations of archetypal patterns in black Americans' quests to change the land where they were forced to live into a home they could claim. The arbitrary barriers to black settlement in the United States begin to break down, and Afro-American identity reinvents itself.

Pilate Dead, one of the principal characters in Toni Morrison's novel *Song of Solomon* (1977), wanders throughout the South after her father's death carrying two important pieces of baggage: a sack of human bones and a geography book. Until she reunites uncomfortably with her prosperous but spiritually bankrupt brother's family and nurtures her nephew, Milkman, who will discover the family's heritage, Pilate will not learn the significance of the bones or the book. Although a fictional character, Pilate reflects the very real dilemma black American writers have faced in resolving their sense of homelessness or in exploring the often puzzling relation between land and family. Claude McKay concludes his autobiography, *A Long Way from Home,* by referring to himself as a "troubadour wanderer" (354). My interest lies in examining how some black writers find resting places for the "bones" they carry (both living and dead) in their alternative spaces of refuge and revitalization. Three figures of landscape appear in the literature over time with such regularity that they become the primary images of a literal and figurative geography in the search for self and home: the wilderness, the underground, and the mountaintop.

During slavery blacks depicted the wilderness as a place of refuge beyond the restricted world of the plantation. As they exhorted each other through song, "Jesus call you, go in de wilderness / To wait upon the Lord." The oral tradition, transmitting folk wisdom and religion, was the medium through which slaves contemplated the Blakean fearful symmetry of the woods as well as its harbor for spiritual reflection. The woods or the swamps were regular sites for religious meetings and conversion experiences in which slaves attained important levels of spiritual mobility. Once this covert model for spiritual elevation, release, and self-esteem was established, slaves were more readily able to envision and often secure physical mobility. Escaping North to free territory or overt resistance to slavery usually started with flight deep into the woods. Slaves narratives by Henry Bibb, William and Ellen Craft, William Wells Brown, and others affirm the effect of such a place on their transforming journey to freedom. When slaves sang, "I'm so glad I come out de wilderness" (sometimes via the underground railroad), they were celebrating this achievement, as if the act of singing could produce this change. Chapter 1 examines how slave songs and narratives enabled language to initiate performance and transformation.

The underground, the region in slave songs that lies "down in the lonesome valley" where individual strength is tested and autonomy achieved, becomes, in modern texts, a stage for self-creating performances and for contact with black culture. In Jean Toomer's *Cane,* Kabnis descends into Fred Halsey's cellar and confronts Father John, a figure of the slave past. In Claude McKay's *Banjo,* Ray fulfills his ambition to be a writer only after he gets "down" with black men from all parts of the African diaspora in the bawdy "Ditch" of Marseilles. These texts are discussed in chapter 2.

Chapter 3 examines how more contemporary writers explore the psychological dimensions that reverse spatial values and invert directions for upward mobility. In his rarely discussed novella, "The Man Who Lived Underground," Richard Wright begins his search for a textual home that he later finds in his autobiography, *Black Boy.* My argument also places this story in a contrasting, yet intertextual, relationship to Ralph Ellison's story "Flying Home" (which has often been neglected by critics in favor of *Invisible Man*) and to LeRoi Jones's play *Dutchman,* where the drama unfolds on an underground train about to derail.

At this point readers may be tempted to see underground settings as a domain for male writers. Chapter 4, however, examines how women writers such as Zora Neale Hurston, Alice Walker, and Gayl Jones construct "womanist" spaces to redirect the conventional search for home. The lowlands imagined in Janie Starks's journey from a porch in Georgia to the muck of the Florida Everglades in *Their Eyes Were Watching God* uncover the roads to self-mastery followed by subsequent women protagonists.

The mountaintop, the biblical Mt. Pisgah empowering the Moses of the spirituals and the quest motif in Martin Luther King, Jr.'s speech, is the third principal space and is discussed in chapters 5 and 6. Here protagonists transcend identity through self-mastery. John Grimes, in James Baldwin's *Go Tell It on the Mountain,* tests his newly acquired manhood against his father's cruelty and arrogance when he undergoes conversion on the powerful threshing floor of a Pentecostal church. And when Pilate Dead, long the weary traveler in Morrison's novel, finally buries the bones on a hilltop, she and Milkman experience the exhilarating magic of flight. "If you surrendered to the air," Morrison concludes teasingly, "you could ride it" (337).

The wilderness, the underground, and the mountaintop are broad geographical metaphors for the search, discovery, and achievement of self. They shape Afro-American literary history from texts that locate places for physical and spiritual freedom (as seen in the episode of wilderness escape in slave narratives and songs), texts that establish place as a stage for performance (speech acts or behavior emanating from "underground" shelters), and texts that shape such performances into celebrations of self. Spatial relations in character development and narrative strategy culminate in Toni Morrison's novel, which takes readers to the mountaintop and far beyond. For *Song of Solomon* examines the requirements and rewards not only of flight from the mountain, but also the riding out and triumph over whatever wilderness impedes our necessary surrender to the air.

Men- and Women-of-Words: From Place to Performance

More than merely describing place, Afro-American writers have vigorously analyzed what kind of behavior or performance occurs in alternative spaces and leads to control over self and environment. Writers and protagonists stake their claim to a culture that sustains individual and group identity. Passage into the alternative space is but one step toward the recovery of wholeness. Writers depict place and performance to set the narrative in motion and encourage reader participation. The open-ended structure and ironic closure in many texts under discussion invite readers to complete performances in and of the narrative. The roles of reader and protagonist are closely linked. Milkman, for example, must *sing* the song of Solomon to comfort Pilate at the moment of her death and to steel himself against his friend-turned-adversary, Guitar. Janie Starks must *tell* the story of her life and loves to Pheoby in an extended oral performance to ensure her heroic posture in the tale Pheoby will relate to others. Wright's underground man, Fred Daniels, *types* his name as well as the opening lines of his story on a stolen typewriter to reaffirm his conquest of geography and identity in the narrative. In each case, a protagonist attempts to read his culture, understand its signs, even create them at the very moment the general reader is engaged in the text. Recall how Ellison's narrator in *Invisible Man* subverts the reader's comfortable distance from the text when he boasts, "Who knows but that, on the lower frequencies, I speak for you?" (439). Consider Morrison's frequent ambiguous closure in novels, or her admission that her language "has to have holes and spaces so the reader can come into it. He or she can feel something visceral, see something striking" (Tate, 125).

5

Scholars of oral literatures and cultures, anthropologists mostly, have isolated performance as a key to differentiating oral from written texts. Studies have found oral tradition in Africa to be more akin to music and dance than to literature, for these art forms exist only as they are actualized through repeated performances. A teller of tales usually formulates his material on a specific occasion and encourages audience participation, which has a determining effect on text and performance. Studies of New World black cultures have affirmed the vitality of ethnographic oral communication linking speech and action. Richard Bauman has defined patterns of performance in verbal art that encourage the performer to be accountable to an audience "for the way in which communication is carried out . . . beyond its referential content." The audience, for its part, evaluates the "relative skill and effectiveness of the performer's display of competence" (11). Performance requires skillful display by the performer and urges evaluation and often participation by the audience. In Roger D. Abrahams's view of performance the key figures are men-of-words, "good talkers and good arguers" (xv), whose tale-telling, gossiping, talking broad, or talking sweet become tests of verbal skill earning reputation and respect.

Scholars have recently applied performance theory to Afro-American prose and drama. Genevieve Fabre has shown how black American drama develops a theater based in quotidian lifestyles and participatory rituals involving verbal repartee; all influence the way dramatic texts are composed. Robert Stepto has demonstrated how narrative strategies become voice-authenticating events that turn ordinary speakers into "articulate heroes" (171). Many of these ideas have contributed to the way I view the protagonists in the literature under discussion as men- and women-of-words engaged in verbal performances *in* narratives that help authors produce performances *of* narratives. I aim to show how these protagonists, beyond achieving literacy, enlarge their range of verbal invention by turning figures of the landscape into settings for the performance of identity. The relations between place and performance thus expand the parameters of language-based criticism of Afro-American fiction and literary history.

From the struggling poets Kabnis and Ray to storyteller Janie Starks and gospel singer Arthur Montana, men- and women-of-words have performed on various stages in the wilderness, the underground, or on the mountaintop to regain self-mastery and to renegotiate the terms of their belonging to a specific community or culture. As Dominique Zahan has observed, among the Bantu of southwestern Africa "the mastery of the self goes together with the conquest of space" (57). The same can be demonstrated closer to home. Geographical settings for cultural performances offer readers a network of links that cohere tradition among such diverse authors as writers of slave narratives, who explored and were tested by an actual wilderness; Harlem Renaissance authors like Jean Toomer and Claude McKay, who imagined premodernist underworld regions as a locus of black cultural consciousness; and Ellison, Wright, Jones, and Hurston, who cultivated the more psychological terrain bordering race and gender. This brings us to the corrective figure of the mountain, a revision and inversion of the underground, offered as Baldwin's and Morrison's stage for self-performance and self-achievement. The shouts of approbation and participation that greeted Martin Luther King, Jr.'s last moving words find an enduring echo in the places and performances these authors have reached by riding out the various forms of oppression threatening to silence us all.

Go in the
Wilderness

CHAPTER ONE

We'll stand the storm:
Slave Songs and Narratives

O black and unknown bards of long ago
How came your lips to touch the sacred fire?
— James Weldon Johnson

The earliest and most significant forms of oral and written Afro-American expression are slave songs and narratives. Together they comprise the beginning of tradition in Afro-American literary history. The songs, commonly called Negro spirituals, reveal the slave's syncretism of Protestant Christianity with various traditional African religious beliefs. They communicate the slave's assessment of the peculiar institution and his search for freedom in this world. The narratives, written by former, sometimes fugitive slaves, present individual and group history as well as arguments against slavery itself. In both voices from the slave community, we discover images of physical and spiritual landscapes, interpretations of history, and heroic characters unlike any in American literature.

Early studies of this material as literature or history did not consider its distinctive cultural base. Marion Starling has argued that slave narratives are works of "sub-literary quality," whose chief importance lies in "their generic relationship to the popular slave novels of the 1850s" (5), most notably Harriet Beecher Stowe's *Uncle Tom's Cabin.* Historians, until recently, have ignored narratives because of their supposedly "unreliable" subjectivity. Scholars such as Charles Nichols, Eugene Genovese, and John Blassingame, however, have restored narratives to their rightful place as primary documents of the slave's past. Lawrence Levine has argued that "slavery was never so complete a system of psychic assault that it prevented slaves from carving out independent cultural forms" (161) that preserve a degree of autonomy and offer a range of positive self-concepts. The system of meaning allowing for this range remains to be studied.

Both narratives and songs are seminal to the development of Afro-American autobiography, fiction, and poetry. Narratives first appeared in print in the early eighteenth century and influenced later autobiographies such as Booker T. Washington's in 1901. The first collection of slave songs was compiled by William Francis Allen, Charles Pickard Ware, and Lucy McKim Garrison and published as *Slave Songs of the United States* (1867). Notable among later collections is James Weldon Johnson and J. Rosamond Johnson's *Book of American Negro Spirituals* (1925). The songs discussed in this chapter are taken from the Johnson and Allen collections. Due to the improvisational nature of composition and the frequent oral transmission of the songs, no texts are definitive. Many verses to a particular song were added, deleted, or changed as the occasion required. Benjamin Mays called the songs a "mass" literature (1), and J. Saunders Redding described them as a "literature of necessity" (3). How the songs and the narratives communicated the slave's view of the world in images of place, identity, and survival is the subject of this chapter.

Christian imagery in the songs and narratives has led some critics to label this literature as naive, childlike, and otherworldly. Closer examination of the texts of the songs and the formal structures of the narratives, however, reveals that slaves appropriated a religious vocabulary for communication more than for belief. Revolutionary sentiments and plans for escape and insurrection were often couched in the religious imagery available to slaves who had few terms to use as weapons against despair and moral degradation. The ideas in this literature reached the masses of slaves primarily through the "invisible" church within the slave community, most often through the words of those anonymous men and women who preached, testified, and told God all their troubles.

Touching the Sacred Fire: Moral Geography in Slave Songs

Among the forty-three songs in the 1867 collection of Negro spirituals is "Go in de Wilderness," collected by Charles Pickard Ware at St. Helena, one of the Port Royal Islands off the coast of South Carolina. The text reads as follows:

12

If you want to find Jesus, go in de wilderness
Go in de wilderness, go in de wilderness.
Mournin' brudder, go in de wilderness
I wait upon de Lord.

Successive verses address figures such as "weepin' Mary," " 'flicted sister," "backslider," and the "half-done Christian." The song admonishes them to seek religion or be converted in "de wilderness," that zone of trial and deliverance beyond the plantation. American readers now had a glimpse of the music and text that James Weldon Johnson would describe as revealing "the group wisdom," "the group philosophy of life" articulated by black and unknown bards. The ideas of conversion in this and other songs may not appear unique, for many religious texts—songs, prayers, and sermons— exhort listeners to experience transcendent grace in retreat from society. In the woods or in nature one may experience salvation. What is significant for slave singers is that their language called into being a place beyond the confines of the plantation where they might undergo a fundamental change in self-perception and moral status.

The songs tell us much about the singer's creative response to the physical and spiritual landscape of slavery. The words and music bring forth an African sensibility in the New World; they offer us evidence of how slaves adapted to a new environment and developed a verbal art that demanded a hearing. Frederick Douglass, in the course of writing his 1845 narrative and as we read it today, reminds us of the emotional power of the songs; the spontaneous tears that interrupt his writing (and our reading) betray the songs' enduring presence as well as their power to bridge dis- tances in time and space. The legacy of the songs and their often ambiguous meaning have haunted and nourished black writers over time. The lyrical images of place and person reverberate in blues melodies for Ralph Ellison's invisible man and in the freedom songs that propel Alice Walker's Meridian through the South, offer sexual solace for Gayl Jones's Ursa Corregidora, and articulate folk heritage for Toni Morrison's Milkman Dead. Negro spirituals contain the seeds of the broad range of images about home, self, and deliverance that have preoccupied writers since enslaved Africans first voiced their claim to blood and kinship in this land.

Although much has been written about the origin of slave songs, includ- ing a debate over the derivation of some texts, few conclusions have been drawn. That the spirituals clearly share a common vocabulary with Methodist and Baptist hymns does not detract from their fundamental difference in meaning and use of language. One area of proof can be seen in the stark contrast between the truncated religious instruction slaves most often received and the broad, aggressive theology they developed to address their needs. My goal here is to analyze the slave's metaphorical and rhythmic use of language that thwarts the dehumanizing effects of slavery by depicting alternative spaces and personae slaves could assume. The songs helped slaves to reconstruct rather than deconstruct culture through language; environments became homes, journeys were undertaken, art was created.

This reconstruction of self and space occurs principally through language. The singer creates an aural space around him, defining a stage that is both communal and individual. The singer sets his voice in motion and draws an assembly about him. Listeners, who usually participate in the call and response structure of the music, are often included in the act and composition of the song. The singer journeys outside himself to others and to the listening space both occupy. The pace of the song as well as its onomatopoeia may well bring about the desired act of deliverance: "Yeddy ole Egyp' dere yowlin'."

The singing of a song also constructs a place to be reached by more direct means. This perhaps explains why Milkman Dead in Morrison's *Song of Solomon* learns of his ancestry through the activity of the singing children at play; or why an enigmatic Louis Armstrong blues stanza spirals the invisible man down into "the blackness of blackness"; why Clay in Jones's *Dutchman* must sing his blues to Lula, even though it brings about his death; why music unites the vagabonds in *Banjo;* or why Ralph Kabnis fears the church songs and shouts in *Cane* that urge him to act upon his fate.

Music creates a landscape, defines a space and a territory the singer and protagonist can claim. The slave songs initiate pilgrimages and other self-creating acts, including resistance and escape, that ultimately defeat the inertia of place and identity upon which the institution of slavery had thrived. By seizing alternatives through poetry and music, slaves charted journeys to many kinds of freedom. The symbolic geography in the slave's religion told where and how to reach the territory of freedom.

Slavery magnified the wretchedness most people feel when they face the reality and burden of human mortality. Religious conversion to the church that blacks built upon the rock of traditional African religion and evangelical Christianity offered some relief by defining an inner cult of believers, an in-group morality that addressed these concerns:

O wretched man that I am
O wretched man that I am
O wretched man that I am
Who will deliver poor me?

I am bowed down with a burden of woe
I am bowed down with a burden of woe
I am bowed down with a burden of woe
Who will deliver poor me?

Recognition of one's wretchedness as a slave, a realization that one is different and deprived, was often the first step in the socioreligious mobility the slave community offered to its believers. The spiritual mobility established in the slave's conversion to the inner morality became the philosophical model for further initiation into free status and a new identity. The initial recognition of wretchedness voiced in the songs became a structural device for organizing personal history in the narratives. "I was born a slave," wrote Linda Brent (a.k.a. Harriet Brent Jacobs), "but I never knew it till six years of happy childhood had passed away. . . . When I was six years old, my mother died; and then for the first time, I learned by the talk around me, that I was a slave" (3,5). Henry Bibb of Kentucky admitted to knowing "nothing of my condition as a slave" until he discovered that his wages were being spent for the education of his white playmate. "It was then I first commenced seeing and feeling that I was a wretched slave" (64-65). Many narratives, like the one by Thomas Jones, began with this point of self-awareness: "I was born a slave. My recollections of early life are associated with poverty, suffering and shame. I was made to feel in my boyhood's first experience that I was inferior and degraded and that I must pass through life in a dependent and suffering condition" (5).

In an effort to assuage individual loneliness and despair, slaves united under the possibility of attaining salvation or freedom. Using the Bible as a source of myth and history, they came to identify with the children of Israel. But they went one step further: they viewed their quotidian experiences as capable of producing apocalyptic change.

The God dat lived in Moses' time
Is just de same today.

My Lord's gonna rain down fire
One of these days, hallelujah!

The historical moment for slaves was never abstract, but imminent. The time for deliverance and witness was always now: "time is a-coming that the sinner must die." Conversion emphasized an individual's recognition of his need for deliverance from sin, which was often described as another form of bondage.

> Jordan deep, Jordan wide
> None don't cross but the sanctified.
>
> Soon as you cease from your sins
> Train goin' to stop and take you in.
>
> I'm goin' away to leave you
> I'm goin' away to leave you
> Sinner, I'm goin' away to leave you
> And I can't stay here.

Salvation offered refuge: "I got a home where the gambler can't go." By experiencing conversion, slaves could change their status from sinner to saved and enter a holy alliance with others and with an avenging deity:

> My God He is a Man—a Man of War,
> An' de Lawd God is His name.
>
> I'm a soljuh in the Army of thuh Lawd,
> I'm a soljuh in this Army.
>
> Hold out your light you heav'n boun' soldier
> Let your light shine around the world.
>
> I'm singing with a sword in mah han' Lord.
> Singing with a sword in mah han'.

Importantly, both salvation and freedom offered a change of identity, signified most dramatically when ex-slaves assumed a different name. Slaves sang, "I tole Jesus be alright / If I change my name." Or,

> If you see my mother, O yes.
> Please tell her for me, O yes.
> That the angels above done change my name,
> And I want to go to heaven in the morning.

William Wells Brown, who was known as Sanford before he escaped to freedom, wrote, "I was not only hunting for my liberty; but also hunting for a name; though I regarded the latter as of little consequence, if I could but gain the former" (218). His successful escape solved this dilemma. There

16

were others: Walton, the slave, became Henry Bibb, the freeman; Olaudah Equiano became Jacob, then Michael, and finally Gustavus Vassa; Arminta Ross became Harriet Tubman; Frederick Augustus Washington Bailey became Frederick Johnson, then Frederick Douglass.

As attractive as this change of identity and name might have been, it could not have happened without the slave's religious survey of the existing environment for alternative landscapes where a new name and a new freedom could be gained. The slave's religion pointed out territories, both physical and spiritual, beyond the reach of the moral, if not the political, authority of the plantation. Yet slaves on the run or hiding in the woods still had to be vigilant against white patrols ("Run nigger run, de patterollers get you"). The notion that another place and identity existed certainly eased the debilitating effects of slavery and solidified a community around a secular theology of freedom: "We were generally a unit and moved together," wrote Frederick Douglass. The physical and spiritual mobility slaves experienced occurred in areas the religion designated as conducive to freedom and salvation, outside the pastoral order, no pun intended, of the plantation. Slaves looked upon nature and determined in their lore that the wilderness, the lonesome valley, and the mountain were places of deliverance. Slave songs pointed out the geography that had to be reached, encountered, sometimes conquered, in order for the new name or the new identity to have effect.

If America, as Leo Marx has argued, "was both Eden and a howling wilderness" (43), slaves developed different ideas about the dichotomy between order and chaos. Slaves knew that as chattel they were considered part of the property and wilds of nature, which a smoothly functioning plantation could restrain. The nearby woods contained enough birds and roaming animals to provide slaves with geographical and naturalistic references for freedom. Henry Bibb, in a letter to his former master Sibley, argued that the freedom to act for oneself is a right "highly appreciated by the wild beasts of the forest and fowls of the air. The terrific screech of the hooting owl is animating to himself and musical to his kind as he goes through the tall forest, from hill top to valley. Not so, with the miserable little screech owl, while he is tied by the leg, or boxed up, in a cage. Though well fed he is made the sport of children" (*Slave Testimony*, hereafter cited as *ST*, 53). Moreover, slaves regarded the "garden" ideal of the plantation with understandable suspicion. Frederick Douglass's description of the Lloyd plantation includes a detailed view of the Great House Farm and the

17

work required to maintain its "large and finely cultivated garden" whose fruits ranged "from the hardy apple of the North to the delicate orange of the South" (39). A tar-covered fence kept out hungry slaves and identified trespassers. Slaves became, Douglass tells us in a brilliant allusion to a common folktale, "as fearful of tar as of the lash" (39). Thus it was hardly a difficult choice for slaves to forsake the pastoral Eden for the unpredictable wilderness. "I felt that my chance was by far better among the howling wolves in the Red River Swamp," wrote Henry Bibb in his narrative, "than before Deacon Whitfield on the cotton plantation" (129). Bibb later boasted in a letter to another master, Gatewood, that several fugitives in Canada "are now the owners of better farms than the men who once owned them" (*ST,* 49).

Slave songs also developed an image of the wilderness as a region preferable to the plantation:

> I found free grace in de wilderness,
> in de wilderness, in de wilderness,
> I found free grace in de wilderness
> For I'm a-going home.

As enslaved Africans began to flee slavery or bury their dead in the New World, the wilderness represented both an area offering passage to home and an enchanted ground affirming the increasingly stronger ties blacks had to the larger landscape:

> Wonder where is my brother gone?
> Wonder where is my brother John?
> He is gone to the wilderness
> Aint comin' no more.
>
> Good mornin' brother pilgrim
> Pray tell me where you bound
> O tell me where you travellin' to
> On-a this enchanted ground.
>
> My name it is poor Pilgrim
> To Canaan I am bound
> Travellin' through this wilderness
> On-a this enchanted ground.

Thus did slaves regularly scrutinize the physical landscape about them.

Although planters often passed along rumors of unspeakable horrors that

18

lay outside the plantation to dissuade blacks from attempting escape, slave lore is filled with geographical references that parallel various states of mind. Here the physical geography links to spiritual landscape; if slaves were considered lowly creatures, for example, they seized upon opportunities to invest that state of being with enough mutability so that changes in the vernacular landscape—hillsides, valleys, swamp land, level ground—became references for the slave's feelings. Slave songs reconstructed the physical environment to find relief from spiritual depression and despair:

> Sometimes I'm up, sometimes I'm down
> O yes Lord
> Sometimes I'm almost to the ground
> O yes Lord.
> Nobody knows the trouble I've seen
> Nobody knows but Jesus
> Nobody knows the trouble I've seen
> Glory Hallelujah.

The slave's recognition of low status, the wretchedness discussed earlier, defined a valley one had to encounter before reaching higher ground:

> You got to walk that lonesome valley
> You got to walk it by yourself
> No one here can walk it for you,
> You got to walk it by yourself.

It was also the individual alone who faced a trial of faith: "Way down yonder by myself / And I couldn't hear nobody pray." And if the sweet chariot were to retrieve the ardent believer, it had to swing "low."

Whereas the valley was an image for conquering despair, the mountain became a figure for personal triumph and witness; the singer, delivered out of bondage to sin or to masters, earned a moment of transcendence. He was privileged to inherit and act upon his achievement of grace:

> Wait till I get on the mountaintop
> Goin' to make my wings go flippity-flop.

His voice could broadcast divine messages:

> Go tell it on the mountain
> That Jesus Christ is born.

And he might witness apocalyptic change:

19

> Daniel saw the stone, hewn out the mountain
> Daniel saw the stone, hewn out the mountain
> Daniel saw the stone, hewn out the mountain,
> Tearing down the kingdom of this world.

Most important, he would gain an intimacy with God and acquire whatever possessions were due him, including self-possession:

> Up on the mountain when my Lord spoke
> Out of his mouth came fire and smoke.
> Looked all around me, it looked so fine,
> And I asked my Lord, if all were mine.

The spirituals thus offer three distinct places of alternative refuge where new identities could be found: the wilderness, the lonesome valley, and the mountaintop. With the discovery of a geography of grace came a strict morality to which the narratives by fugitive slaves offer additional testimony. The spirituals examine acts that bring about conversion or create a new identity (*walking* the lonesome valley, *singing* with a sword in the hand); they are acts of language that initiate performances of freedom in alternative spaces of refuge. The narratives examine further the relation of place and performance by detailing the personal knowledge, courage, and self-confidence that deliverance required.

Standing the Storm: Slave Narratives and the Test of Wilderness

Just as the singers of slave songs imagined the wilderness as a metaphorical place of refuge and conversion, authors of slave narratives accorded considerable importance to geography. Some narrators were quick to describe their condition as "wretched"; others saw themselves so closely linked to the southern landscape that they sought to control geography and identity through their use of language. If the songs argued that the difference between slavery and freedom was more a matter of geography than of human flaw or racial predisposition, the narrators showed how control of an environment could lead to a control of self and personal destiny. The effect of such reasoning can be seen in Frederick Douglass's 1845 narrative, which continues to dazzle critics by the author's sustained artistry and verbal dexterity, both of which are tools for Douglass to measure and present his life.

The opening sentence reveals Douglass's subtle equation between geography and identity. "I was born in Tuckahoe," he begins, yet he goes on to accumulate such precise cartographical detail that the sentence demonstrates how the narrative will assume authority over place and voice. To the exact mile does Douglass situate himself and the reader to show the extent of his knowledge, his ability to reason, and, in short, his intelligence. Articulating *where* he is becomes Douglass's way of knowing and presenting *who* he is. The full sentence reads, "I was born in Tuckahoe, near Hillsborough, and about twelve miles from Easton, in Talbot County, Maryland" (23). Douglass's use of geography here accomplishes two purposes: first, his control of language, as a demonstration of knowledge, compensates for the lack of conventional personal information that slavery denied him and that readers of autobiography expect: family and age. Douglass admits, "I have no accurate knowledge of my age" (23), and he must speculate about his parentage. Second, his awareness of identity through geography, or environment, differentiates him from the animal imagery slavery bestowed upon him: "Slaves know as little of their ages as horses know of theirs" (23). Denied the conventional measures of identity through age or heredity, Douglass constructs alternative means to define his humanity. He sets up a dichotomy between place and person: the place that denies him humanity is described and recreated through the exercise of an intelligence that is the unmistakable sign of humanness. Douglass thus locates himself and the reader in time and space. This moment of reckoning and reasoning is the key to the way Douglass and other former slave narrators extricate themselves from the place that conspires to keep them ignorant and bestial.

Douglass further observes the link between geography and identity when he relates the change in status accorded to his master Captain Anthony Auld, whose "title," Douglass surmises, was "acquired by sailing a craft in the Chesapeake Bay" (27). Readers are not surprised later when Douglass apostrophizes ships in the same bay to carry him to freedom. Douglass finally escapes from slavery by impersonating a sailor, and the title he earns upon crossing the bay is that of freedman. Douglass may have shared a brief moment of delight through a ruse such as that enjoyed by Jackson Whitney who wrote to his former master, William Riley, that "I thought it was time for me to make my feet feel for Canada and let your conscience feel in your pocket" (*ST,* 114).

Douglass's awareness of slavery grows when he discovers that literacy is the ultimate tool to self-possession. Reading also increases the range of his geographical references to slavery in a strange land he has yet to make his own: "The more I read, the more I was led to abhor and detest my enslavers. I could regard them in no other light than a band of successful robbers, who had left their *homes,* and gone to *Africa,* and stolen us from our *homes* and in a strange *land* reduced us to slavery" (67, emphasis mine). This knowledge returns Douglass to the feelings he will have in common with slave singers and other narrators, "a view of my wretched condition, without the remedy." Furthermore, it "opened my eyes to the horrible pit, but to no ladder upon which to get out" (67). Translated into the language of the slave songs, Douglass is trapped in the lonesome valley without a way to the mountaintop. The pit is not only Douglass's experience of imprisoning slavery, but also the locus of his awareness of slavery; it is not the refuge we shall see in later works by McKay or Wright, but a place Douglass creates out of his longing for freedom as revealed by the *height* of his intelligence: "Freedom now appeared, to disappear no more forever. . . . It looked from every star, it smiled in every calm, breathed in every wind, and moved in every storm" (68). The storm Douglass and other slaves were willing to stand came with their escape from the dehumanizing order of the plantation and into the grueling, unpredictable, yet promising test of wilderness.

Fugitive slaves were often poorly equipped with nothing but a belief in God and the hope that the North Star would be visible. Henry Bibb and others often had to avoid public roads. "I travelled all that day square off from the road through the wild forest without any knowledge of the country whatever for I had nothing to travel by but the sun by day, and the moon and stars by night" (146). When slaves escaped in groups, they often chose a minister to lead them, thereby making more concrete the relationship between religion and the search for freedom. One preacher, a Methodist, tried to persuade John Thompson to join his band of runaways, but Thompson had yet to be converted:

> The Methodist preacher . . . urged me very strongly to accompany them, saying that he had full confidence in the surety of the promises of God . . . he believed he was able to carry him safely to the land of freedom, and accordingly he was determined to go. Still I was afraid to risk myself on such uncertain promises; I dared not trust an unseen God.
> On the night on which they intended to start . . . they knelt in prayer to the great God of Heaven and Earth, invoking Him to guard them . . . and go with them to their journey's end. (76)

22

Later, when he was saved from a dangerous situation, Thompson joined God's army. He offered this witness of his conversion and his pilgrimage into the wilderness:

> I knew it was the hand of God, working in my behalf; it was his voice warning me to escape from the danger towards which I was hastening. Who would not praise such a God? Great is the Lord, and greatly to be praised.
>
> I felt renewed confidence and faith, for I believed that God was in my favor, and now was the time to test the matter . . . I fell on my knees, and with hands uplifted to high heaven, related all the late circumstances to the Great King, saying that the whole world was against me without a cause, besought his protection, and solemnly promised to serve him all the days of my life. I received a spiritual answer of approval; a voice like thunder seeming to enter my soul, saying, I am your God and am with you; though the world be against you, I am more than the world; though wicked men hunt you, trust in me, for I am the Rock of your Defense. . . . I praised God at the top of my voice. . . . I retired to my hiding place in the woods. (80-81)

Black religion's call into "de wilderness" told slaves where to seek salvation and liberation, there to be tested, tried, and "be baptized." Religion agitated the slave's search. Some preachers like Nat Turner and Denmark Vesey actually planned insurrections. Turner frequently hid in the woods where he communed with the Spirit and received assurance that his struggle had divine sanction: "I saw white spirits and black spirits engaged in battle, and the sun was darkened—the thunder rolled in the heaven, and blood flowed in streams—and I heard a voice saying, 'Such is your luck, such you are called to see, and let it come rough or smooth, you must surely have it.' . . . After this revelation in the year of 1825 . . . I sought more than ever to obtain true holiness before the great day of judgement should appear, and then I began to receive the true knowledge of faith" (136). The night of his insurrection in Southampton, Virginia, Turner went again to the woods, this time with his co-conspirators. They shared cider and roast pork as a sacrament to their mission.

Other slaves often secreted themselves in the woods, if only to meditate on their condition. The wilderness revealed man's place in the natural harmony of the world. As Henry Bibb reflected: "I thought of the fishes of the water, the fowls of the air, the wild beasts of the forest, all appeared to be free to go where they pleased, and I was an unhappy slave" (72). Nature offered examples of the harmony of life similar to those in traditional African religious thought; for enslaved Africans the wilderness in America simply offered another covenant between man and God. Frederick Douglass once described this communion: "I was in the wood, buried in its somber gloom and hushed in its solemn silence, hidden from all human eyes, shut in with nature and with nature's God, and absent from all human contrivances. Here was a good place to pray, to pray for help, for deliverance" (*Life and Times,* 135).

Following the call into the wilderness was Henry Bibb standing on a bluff overlooking the Ohio River, perhaps knowing then that in African beliefs water, as well as the wilds, was a place of divine power; spirits were known to inhabit wells, springs, rivers, and streams. There Bibb mused: "Oh that I had the wings of a dove, that I might soar away to where there is no slavery; no clanking of chains, no captives, no lacerating of backs, no parting of husbands and wives; and where man ceases to be the property of his fellow man" (72). With similar zeal Frederick Douglass called to the Chesapeake, "This very bay shall yet bear me into freedom" (*Life and Times,* 125). Even the most servile of bondsmen, Josiah Henson, whom Harriet Beecher Stowe used as the prototype for Uncle Tom, felt compelled to find freedom in the North: "Once to get away, with my wife and children, to some spot where I could feel that they were indeed *mine* —where no grasping master could stand between me and them, as arbiter of their destiny—was a heaven yearned after with insatiable longing" (60-61). And Henry "Box" Brown's revelation told him how he could escape successfully: "I prayed fervently that he who seeth in secret and knew the inmost desires of my heart would lend me his aid in bursting my fetters asunder and in restoring me to possession of those rights of which men had robbed me; when suddenly, the idea flashed across my mind of shutting myself *up in a box,* and getting myself conveyed as dry goods to a free state" (194).

The impulse to gain freedom was also the beginning of a change in the slave's character. He began to strengthen himself for the difficulties he would have to endure. Gustavus Vassa, one of the few narrators who vividly remembered his former life in Africa, wrote that in the midst of meditating on ending his enslavement, he resolved to use "every honest means and all that was possible on my part to obtain it" (87). James W. C. Pennington, a fugitive blacksmith, had a very realistic idea of the trials before him: "I considered the difficulties of the way—the reward that would be offered— the human bloodhounds that would be set upon my track—the weariness—

the hunger—the gloomy thought of not only losing all one's friends in one day, but of having to seek and make new friends in a strange world. . . . But, as I have said, the hour was come, and the man must act or forever be a slave" (216).

The decision to act was sometimes taken in flight from cruel treatment. William Parker fought back when his master tried to whip him: "I let go of my hold—bade him goodbye, and ran for the woods. As I went by the field, I beckoned to my brother, who left work and joined me at a rapid pace." Parker's bid for autonomy was doubly important for it came as he was approaching adulthood:

> Although upon the threshold of manhood, I had, until the relation with my master was sundered, only dim perceptions of the responsibilities of a more independent position. I longed to cast off the chains of servitude because they chafed my free spirit, and because I had a notion that my position was founded in injustice. . . . The impulse to freedom lends wings to the feet, buoys up the spirit within, and the fugitive catches glorious glimpses of light through rifts and seams in the accumulated ignorance of his years of oppression. How briskly we traveled on that eventful night and the next day! (290, 291)

So strong was the impulse to escape in Henry Bibb that he "learned the art of running away to perfection." He did so regularly until he finally broke "the bonds of slavery and landed myself in Canada where I was regarded as a man and not as a thing" (165).

Fugitive slaves on the run had to be constantly on their guard. The test of the wilderness was primarily a struggle for survival; it required a code of situational ethics that sanctioned a range of behavior that included stealing food, helping others, or commiting murder, which the gun-toting Harriet Tubman threatened to do ("Dead niggers tell no tales"). More important, the fugitive had to take an active role in his search for deliverance; he had to find help along the arduous road and to confront the basic ambiguity of the wilderness that could help or hinder his efforts. William Wells Brown distrusted blacks as well as whites. "The slave is brought up to look upon every white man as an enemy," Brown admitted. "And twenty-one years in slavery had taught me that there were traitors, even among colored people" (216). John Thompson used his newly embraced Christianity as a criterion in seeking help. In one instance he was directed to a house occupied by a certain Mrs. R., "a free woman, and one of *God's true children*" (85, emphasis mine). Fugitives also had to recognize the basic duality in nature; the same natural force, such as a wide river, deep valley, soggy swamp, treacherous storm, or impassable mountain, was both obstacle and aid. It was the fugitive's skillful behavior, action, and courage to confront the wilderness that turned potentially hazardous situations into conquests. The wilderness thus became an important test of man's faith in himself and in God's power to bring deliverance or free territory within reach. This was how man *joined* himself with God, with nature, and how he *earned* his freedom.

Henry Bibb structured his entire narrative around this test of wilderness. Once he had escaped to free territory, he returned to rescue his wife and child, but the attempt failed. He then escaped alone. Each time he renewed his covenant with divine forces, passing "the night in prayer to our Heavenly Father, asking that He would open to me even the smallest chance for escape" (96). With his wife and child Bibb encountered nature at its harshest level, making

> our way down to Red River swamps among the buzzing insects and wild beasts of the forest. We wandered about in the wilderness for eight or ten days. . . . Our food was parched corn . . . but most of the time, while we were out, we were lost. We wanted to cross the Red River but could find no conveyance to cross it.
>
> I recollect one day of finding a crooked tree which bent over the river. . . . We crossed over on the tree. . . . We made our bed that night in a pile of dry leaves. . . . We were much rest-broken, wearied from hunger and travelling through briers, swamps and cane breaks. (125–26)

Then they met wolves, howling and close upon them, propelling Bibb into a brave performance:

> The wolves kept howling. . . . I then thought that the hour of death for us was at hand . . . for there was no way for our escape. My little family were looking up to me for protection, but I could afford them none. . . . I was offering up my prayers to that God who never forsakes those in the hour of danger who trust in him. . . . I was surrounded by those wolves. But it seemed to be the will of a merciful providence that our lives should be spared, and that we should not be destroyed by them. I rushed forth with my bowie knife in hand. . . . I made one desperate charge at them . . . making a loud yell at the top of my voice, that caused them to retreat and scatter which was equivalent to a victory on our part. Our prayers were answered. . . . The next morning there were no wolves to be seen or heard. (126–28)

Bibb's performance met one of the tests of wilderness: that man act upon his faith and participate in his own deliverance. The reward for his behavior was not only access to free territory, but also the acquisition of a new name, a new identity.

The Reverend Thomas Jones experienced a similar confrontation with nature and turned it to his advantage through prayer and performance. Just as he was about to be deported by a ship's captain who discovered him as a stowaway, stormy seas and then favorable tides made it possible for Jones to take to the water: "a severe storm came on and for several days we were driven by the gale. I turned to and cooked for the crew. The storm was followed by a calm of several days; and then the wind sprung up again and the Captain made for port at once. . . . while the Captain was in the city . . . I made a raft of loose board as I could get and hastily bound them together, and committing myself to God, I launched forth upon the waves. The shore was about a mile distant; I had the tide in my favor" (46).

By most accounts the test of wilderness, with its threat of death and promise of rebirth, offered hope to those who saw themselves as among the chosen people. But deliverance from slavery, passage into and out of the wilderness, was conditioned on man's trial, his willingness to be struck dead to sin, to slavery, to the order of the plantation. Also tested was his ability to confront his own despair, fear, and solitude, which could earn him a new identity.

Thus as early as the period of slavery did known and unknown bards devise ways in which a free black identity could take root in America. The literature and lore blacks created, the songs and narratives, depict what transformations of place and person held sway in the antebellum imagination. Against the constricting space for personal growth that was the plantation, singers and writers established alternative places of refuge, regeneration, and performance that would ensure deliverance from bondage.

Slave songs, as we have seen, outlined elements of a religious and secular conversion that made spiritual mobility and change in moral status possible. The narratives recounted tales of personal valor that effected physical mobility out of the environment of slavery. Taken together, these texts lay bare the broad geography of the wilderness, the lonesome valley, and the mountaintop as landscapes for self-fulfillment. The songs identified the wilderness as a separate area with its own boundaries and dualistic characteristics; the narratives gave greater emphasis to escape experiences and showed how the wilderness was a point of passage into tests of nature, earning defeat or deliverance. As Afro-American literature develops more formal structures of autobiography, fiction, and poetry, we shall see writers returning to this richly complex and vibrant lore for images of land where black men and women connect to a sometimes submerged culture that can make them whole. Protagonists and authors, however, will assume much artistic freedom by either accepting or rejecting the demands this landscape and cultural awareness make upon them. Jean Toomer and Claude McKay, as we shall see, touch a similar base but for different purposes. Ralph Kabnis's swan song in Toomer's *Cane* becomes a unifying jazz composition in McKay's *Banjo*, the lonesome valley an underground for nations stirring awake.

Down in the
Lonesome Valley

CHAPTER TWO

To wake the nations underground: Jean Toomer and Claude McKay

> In time, for though the sun is setting on
> A song-lit race of slaves, it has not set.
> — Jean Toomer

The gift of song and the prevalence of freedom-directed narratives charted Afro-American cultural geography within and without the slave community. Following Emancipation the same cultural and literary forms told black writers where to seek their heritage. Some early writers, such as Charles Chesnutt, were successful in conveying the ironic twist in black folk expressions. Others, like Paul Laurence Dunbar, borrowed selectively. Dunbar used the double-edged voice found in early slave sermons in his poem "Antebellum Sermon," but in most of his work he strayed too close to projecting apologist stereotypes common to the plantation tradition in American literature. The possibilities for social advancement that came with Emancipation invited multiple responses to examining role and place in society.

Writers began to experiment more with language and literature. James Weldon Johnson and William E. B. Du Bois invented upon the interplay between folk and standard forms of speech, music, and art. Johnson's nameless protagonist in the novel *The Autobiography of an Ex-Coloured Man* (1912) attempted to forge a new American art by merging ragtime and classical music. He was adept at neither and retreated cowardly from the cultural and personal demands of serious art: he had to accept the blackness he had too quickly renounced. Du Bois merged fiction, social commentary, song, and poetry in his stirring essay *The Souls of Black Folk* (1903), creating a new form for autobiographical meditation. Both writers signaled a new awakening of black artistic consciousness. Yet it was not until the

31

period of the twenties, the very edge of modernism in visual and literary arts, that writers drew upon the abiding presence of a folk base in art to express the heart of a people. The sun had not yet set on the song-lit race. Paradoxically, the writers who tapped the resonance of the submerged culture and its meaning for blacks during the twentieth century were themselves displaced, alienated wanderers. Jean Toomer and Claude McKay sought to come to terms with the pull of ancestral group identity in their struggles to become writers. Each heard different tunes "Caroling softly souls of slavery" (*Cane,* 21). Each tried to link his voice to the music.

Toomer and McKay were also afflicted with a profound ambivalence about the relationship between their racial identity and artistic calling. McKay, a dark-complexioned Jamaican tried to reconcile intellect, or education, with the raw passion he believed to be primitive. Toomer, a mulatto light enough to pass for white, eventually abandoned his race, but in *Cane* he tried to reconcile detached observation of life, which he preferred, with the participation life demanded in order to give full voice to the people and to himself. The geography in *Cane*'s three-part structure (South-North-South) and in the settings in McKay's trilogy of novels (America-France-Jamaica) suggests both writers' need to examine the impact of place on personality and to reach a cultural ground conducive to self-understanding. Although McKay's novels were not conceived as a trilogy, they do emerge as separate attempts to complete a theme bordering closely on the indeterminacy one finds in *Cane.* West Indian critic Kenneth Ramchand was among the first to see the interrelatedness in McKay's fiction and to encourage intertextual readings.

Both Toomer and McKay chose protagonists to represent their private dilemmas; literature was the proving ground. The West Indian Ray, an aspiring poet, parallels McKay's life and wanderlust; Toomer, as critic Nellie McKay has shown, was more direct in acknowledging his link to Ralph Kabnis: " 'Kabnis' is *Me*" (53). The protagonist in the later part of *Cane* (1923), and something of the observing voice in the early part of the book, Kabnis is a struggling man-of-words. He attempts to embrace the songs of the black peasants and to merge them into his own voice. Yet the "lemon-faced" Kabnis is also terrorized by the demands racial identity makes on him; he is unwilling to carry the full weight and responsibility of racial acceptance. Ray, in McKay's *Home to Harlem* (1928) and *Banjo* (1929), longs to be a singer of tales, a poet who draws inspiration and craft from the common subsoil of the race that nourishes blacks from Africa, the

Caribbean, and the United States. Ray's success is inconclusive. (Does he embrace culture or chaos?) Readers are left with Ray's continuous vagabonding and no real proof of his art. For McKay, it is his female protagonist Bita Plant, in *Banana Bottom* (1933), who actually fulfills Ray's abortive journey. Bita anchors McKay's novels and links them into the trilogy suggested by their common character types and progressive thematic development.

Toomer and McKay, for all their evasiveness and ambivalence, do succeed in crafting a view of landscape and language to alter significantly the map of racial ancestry. They reassess the "wilderness" setting so central to the slave songs and narratives. They enlarge the brooding image of life in the "Black Belt," which Du Bois and Johnson so cautiously recreated, and which Robert Stepto so skillfully examined as symbolic geography. Whatever wilderness now exists is but an intermediary stage one passes through to reach the terrifying but necessary ground beneath behavior (the underground) and the performance of identity. Kabnis feels alienated by the haunting song-filled southern night as much as Ray feels rejected by a class-conscious society. Both attempt to escape these forms of wilderness by getting beneath the chaos to a more private order they can either embrace or reject on their own terms. In the works of both authors a prevalence of burial imagery and acts of descent exists, and deliverance comes through rebirth.

How McKay and Toomer depict the underground will clarify directions other writers will take to encounter the same region, but with more surreal and absurdist perspectives on man's fate, human invisibility, and performance. Toomer and McKay propose a new compass of the imagination, a new way of unearthing and navigating a buried or hidden cultural geography: Toomer provides a simple drawing of geometrical half-circles, or arcs, in the text of *Cane* to preface and shape two areas of cultural and narrative performance as well as to measure their effect; McKay offers an emotionally charged trilogy to examine the necessity of exile and the rewards of return. Together the authors uncover the painful depths of cultural immersion required for the song-lit race of slaves to sing.

Toomer. The Arcs of Indeterminacy: "Soil; and the overarching heavens"

Cane, like Ellison's *Invisible Man,* has inspired a host of critical interpretations, mostly due to Toomer's open-ended lyrical narrative. *Cane* is not a novel as such, but is a collection of poems and prose sketches, teasing us to find some unity and coherence in the work. One kind of unity is geographical: the opening prose-poems and short fiction take place in the rural South where an unnamed, detached observer recounts the lives of women protagonists. The second section occurs in the North and examines with equal perspicacity the alienation and disorientation of men and women in an urban environment. The last section of the book returns readers to the South in the prose-drama of "Kabnis," wherein the title character tries to become the "face of the South" (158) as well as its voice.

Toomer, born into a family of mixed-bloods, embodied indeterminacy. He sojourned among blacks and whites and prided himself on the ambiguity of his racial ancestry until he finally repudiated his blackness. "I am of no field," he wrote later in *Essentials,* a privately printed book of aphorisms, "I am of the field of being." He lived for a short time in the South and felt the powerful sway of its culture. As he revealed in a letter to Claude McKay, then one of the editors of *The Liberator,* Toomer felt drawn "into the Negro group" and loved it: "A visit to Georgia last fall was the starting point of almost everything of worth that I have done. I heard folksongs come from the lips of Negro peasants. I saw the rich dusk beauty that I had heard many false accents about, and of which till then, I was somewhat skeptical. And a deep part of my nature, a part that I had repressed, sprang suddenly to life and responded to them. Now, I cannot conceive of myself as aloof and separated" (*The Wayward and the Seeking,* 18).

Yet, Toomer did not remain long within the race nor champion its cause. Instead, he found in nature an objective correlative for his ambivalence and titled his book accordingly. Natural sugarcane is delicious for the first chews, but once the sweetness has been extracted, it becomes fibrous, bitter.

As slave singers knew, nature could be a help or a hindrance to securing deliverance, to reaching campground, or to riding out the wilderness. The South, the land of cane and ancestral territory for most American blacks, is both a hostile political field and an abundantly fertile cultural terrain. These tensions in nature and in geography match the "warring ideals" of being black and American, which Du Bois called double consciousness. This condition plagued Toomer throughout his life. Writing *Cane* was Toomer's attempt to contain, if not to reconcile, the profound ambivalence attending his racial ambiguity and to emerge like Kabnis from the subsoil or cellar of racial awareness into a bright new day. Kabnis, however, was carrying a bucket of dead coals.

Critical interpretations of the book's ending have engendered two schools of thought: some scholars have viewed Kabnis's descent into and rise from the underground as a positive assertion of himself as a black artist; others have viewed the bucket of dead coals as a signal of Kabnis's ultimate failure. Houston Baker, Jr., Nellie McKay, and others have argued for the first interpretation; Darwin Turner for the latter. Neither perspective is fully correct. Toomer works against too easy a resolution. He forces us to accept the fundamental duality in sugarcane, or in nature, just as he has left us with the uncomfortable duality of his troubled racial identity. The key gesture of performance in *Cane* is Kabnis's emergence from the underground as two images fix in the reader's mind: the dead coals and the new day he faces. The drawing of the two arcs as conflicting halves of an incomplete circle become warring ideals in Toomer's literary double consciousness, charging the book's every scene with electricity.

Toomer's visual arcs—the single half-circles, each prefacing the two major geographical divisions of the text, and the pair held in magnetic tension before the last section, "Kabnis"—introduce the place or landscape of action and the expanding insight of the observing narrator. Movement through space and geography (ascent-descent, South-North) is key to the design and meaning of the book. Toomer's circularity anticipates Ellison's teasing structural metaphor of the boomerang as well as Zora Neale Hurston's geometrical warning that black homelessness, which Toomer knew so well, and black rootlessness, which plagued McKay, can cause things to "come around in queer ways." In a letter to his friend and literary mentor Waldo Frank, Toomer outlined the structure in *Cane:* "From three angles, *Cane*'s design is a circle. Aesthetically, from simple forms to complex forms, and back to simple forms. Regionally, from the South up into the North, and back into the South, and then a return North. From the point of view of spiritual entity behind the work, the curve really starts with Bona and Paul (awakening), plunges into Kabnis, emerges in Karintha, etc. swings around into Theatre and Box Seat, and ends (pauses) in Harvest Song" (Davis, 244). The spatial and spiritual readings of the text intersect. Together they identify the unnamed observer in the early chapters as an incarnation of Paul Johnson (of "Bona and Paul"), who becomes Ralph Kabnis, who then becomes the observer. Toomer's arcs direct us to the way artistic consciousness attempts to incorporate the known with the unknown, and to contain at once two potentially contradictory impulses, levels of consciousness, and places.

Lewis, a visionary like Kabnis and in many ways his alter-ego, accuses Kabnis of failing to realize the fundamental complementarity of opposites, which can help him accept his identity rather than fight it. "Can't hold them can you? Master; slave. Soil; and the overarching heavens. Dusk; dawn" (218). Kabnis's discomfort becomes the reader's privileged insight. At the end of *Cane* readers are meant to hold what Kabnis cannot: two images, two arcs of consciousness. The dead coals of the past must be carried into the promise of the new day. The past informs the present. Although this scene appears at the end of the book, it is not meant to resolve the story, for Toomer's narrative design, like an ever-widening spiral, actually takes us forward to the beginning of *Cane*. The artist's search for place and performance, homeland and heritage as the appropriate stage or setting for his art begins with Paul Johnson of "Bona and Paul."

In this story Paul and Art are college roommates. Paul's race is indeterminate; it is the source of Paul's moody or "moony" disposition and of Art's puzzlement. Before they go out on a double date, Paul sits in his "room of two windows," which represent his dual racial identity, his double consciousness. "Bona," the white girl Paul dates, "is one window. One window, Paul" (137). Through his window Paul has a vision of the South and reflects on its relation to him: "Paul follows the sun to a pine-matted hillock in Georgia. He sees the slanting roofs of gray unpainted cabins tinted lavender." The scene also hints at Paul's racial origin: "A Negress chants a lullaby beneath the mate-eyes of a southern planter." The vision of a possible, though unused, past brings Paul to a glow, a flicker of self-recognition and self-understanding. "Paul follows the sun into himself in Chicago." This glow, however, affects his view through Bona's window. "With his own glow he looks through a dark pane" (137–38), the frame through which Paul sees Bona. The hint of epiphany in Paul's vision of the "hillock in Georgia," shows the dark pane to be Toomer's pun on the pain of darkness falling, like Du Bois's veil of color, between the possible lovers, alienating each from the other and causing Paul's internal discomfort. Yet Bona assumes Paul is black, and she is disappointed when he fails to fit her stereotype of black men: "Colored; cold. Wrong somewhere" (144). Art, on the other hand, feels the stares of people in the Crimson Gardens, the nightclub they attend. He intuits Paul's ill ease and would protect Paul if Paul would only assert himself: "I could stick up for him if he'd only come out, one way or the other and tell a feller" (146). Paul is on the verge of racial awareness, as Kabnis will be, "suspended a few feet above the soil whose touch would resurrect him" (191). But Paul's inability to affirm the identity required in love, sexual compatibility (represented by Bona), or creativity (represented by Art/art) leaves him empty and alone. The Crimson Gardens, a modernist Eden, invites pastoral romance and sexual union, and Paul is tempted. But once he starts to explain his intentions to a black doorman who has aroused his guilt, Paul misses his chance with Bona. Paul's boast that "something beautiful is going to happen. . . . That I am going out and know her whom I brought here with me to these Gardens which are purple like a bed of roses would be at dusk" (152–53) ends in his loss.

A similar situation occurs in "Avey." The nameless narrator puts Avey to sleep with his grandiose, tedious talk about the art he hopes to create, which would "open the way for women the likes of her. . . . I recited some of my own things to her. I sang, with a strange quiver in my voice, a promise song" (87). The speaker is more impressed with the sound of his voice than with fulfilling its promise. Neither he nor Paul consummates his desires. But they do imbibe something of the culture haunting them, no matter how submerged, hidden, or underground it may be. These characters come to represent a familiar type for Toomer.

Similarly, Dan Moore in "Box Seat" follows Toomer's arcs of consciousness into irresolution and indeterminacy. Dan rails against the constraints of middle-class propriety. Unlike Paul, Dan affirms his belonging to "bloodlines that waver South" (119). He proclaims, "I am Dan Moore. I was born in a canefield" (105). He also discovers the location of the submerged culture Toomer believed to be near extinction. When Dan hears the rumble of a passing streetcar, he imagines the subterranean reverberations to be "the mutter of powerful underground races" (108). This realization, however, only partially aids Dan's fight against northern middle-class restrictions on affirming race and sexuality. The theater box seats are prisons. Dan is unable to free his girlfriend Muriel, just as Paul fails to couple with Bona, and as the enthralled speaker fails to possess the elusive Avey. The character who comes closest to merging the arcs or the warring ideals of heritage and double consciousness is Kabnis, who takes the greater risk of entering the underground the other men have only glimpsed. Kabnis not only travels *down* to the South, he also goes beneath the paved streets where Dan heard the rumble of buried races. He gets beneath the "hillock" in Paul's Georgia, and goes right to the damp seediness of Fred Halsey's workshop cellar. There on the underground stage Kabnis enacts the drama of self-realization or self-reckoning. His effort to become the voice of the South produces only stutters. His speech fills with buried or inarticulate sounds from the "Misshapen, split-gut, tortured, twisted words" (224) he utters so fitfully in the presence of Father John. Yet he learns enough to become the detached observer in the rest of *Cane*, particularly in "Karintha," "Becky," "Reapers," and "Blood Burning Moon." If he casts most of the characters in underground situations or in burial imagery, he does so to provoke their rise as well as his own.

Toomer's sketches of southern women, for which *Cane* is best known, are filled with these "split-gut, tortured" words describing the grotesqueries in their "buried" lives. Karintha buries her illegitimate child in a pine forest. Becky, a white woman "with two Negro sons," is banished by the community to a strip of land by the railroad tracks. A scapegoat for the town's racism and hidden envy for her taboo-defying relationships, Becky gets buried alive when the chimney of her house collapses upon her. Carma hides herself in a canefield only to expose the truth of her feigned suicide and real adultery. Fern cloaks her sexual promiscuity with condescension to men, whereas Esther submerges her sexuality under bourgeois propriety and fantasizes about an immaculate conception. Such is Toomer's view — and Kabnis's — of a repressive, terrifying South. Yet the North, with its gated houses, boxed trees, and confining theater box seats, also limits people and distorts nature. The ancestral ground becomes obscured and can be approached only through the imagination. This is Kabnis's double burden, his dual journey to a place of performance and verbal affirmation or denial of identity. Following Toomer's aesthetic or spiritual map into the territory *Cane* uncovers, Kabnis's sojourn underground to what he calls "The Hole" is part of the beginning rather than the end of the book's spiral structure. *Cane* is not the "swan song" Toomer intended, but the beginning of cultural discovery. Exploring the buried lives of black Americans, Toomer stumbles upon a key to waking this nation underground.

Kabnis enters Fred Halsey's cellar, which is the symbolic subsoil of the South, only after he has been terrorized by his misunderstanding of the surface features of the land and community (he fears being lynched or run out of town). He has also transgressed the overly strict rules of the school where he teaches. He flees one imagined confrontation, tramps through mud and dirt, and ends up getting fired from the school where he has taken refuge. Kabnis has actually been trapped in the figurative wilderness of his fear and confusion. He is stripped of his job, his dirty clothes, and his false identity. The naked, childlike Kabnis is ready to be reborn or "baptized" into a new understanding of the South. Fred Halsey gives Kabnis the ritual bath and offers him a home and a position as an apprentice in his wheelwright shop ("Shapin shafts and buildin wagons'll make a man of him what nobody . . . can take advantage of," 188). As Halsey "arranges for the bath before the fire" and "bustles and fusses about Kabnis as if he were a child" (193), Kabnis descends deeper into the culture where his more appropriate education begins.

Halsey's house, in Toomer's landscape, parallels and contrasts with Hanby's school. Both are educational and cultural institutions, yet the school fosters obedience and racial accommodation (a clear analogy to Washington's Tuskegee Institute), while the workshop teaches assertive self-reliance. One rejects Kabnis, the other nurtures him. On the surface Hanby's school is as obsolete as Halsey's trade. A more significant opposition exists between Halsey's house and his workshop. Toomer describes Halsey's parlor as having a "seediness" about it replete with "imitation" bronze candlesticks and fading photographs of several generations of family. The most telling object is "a family clock (not running)" (167). All suggests that time has stopped here. Halsey's workshop similarly reveals little present activity; tools are idle and the one window is in disrepair, "with as many panes broken as whole" (195), which recalls Paul's peering through windows to view an image of his past. Halsey's workshop links to Kabnis's past and to the history of the South. Here Kabnis discovers "The Hole" and old Father John, who lives there.

This cellar or "Hole" houses the underground rumble Dan Moore heard in "Box Seat," and a similar image of Father John, whom Dan saw confined to a wheelchair much like the "high-backed" chair he occupies in "Kabnis." Dan's sympathetic view is rendered in language drawn from the slave songs he's sure the old man remembers, along with the subterranean, ominous "rumblings": "Strange I never really noticed him before. Been sitting there for years. Born a slave. Slavery not so long ago. He'll die in his chair. Swing low, sweet chariot. Jesus will come and roll him down the river Jordan. Oh, come along, Moses, you'll get lost; stretch out your rod and come across. LET MY PEOPLE GO! Old man. Knows every one who passes the corners. Saw the first horse-cars. The first Oldsmobile. And he was born in slavery. . . . He saw Grant and Lincoln. . . . Strange force that drew me to him. . . . I told him to look into the heavens. He did, and smiled. I asked him if he knew what that rumbling is that comes up from the ground" (125).

In an underground without boundaries in both time and space, "huge, limitless in the candle light" (210), Kabnis meets the same Father John. Unlike Dan's song-filled praise Kabnis offers "split-gut" argumentative words: "Slave boy whom some Christian mistress taught to read the Bible. Black man who saw Jesus in the ricefields, and began preaching to his people. Moses- and Christ-words used for songs. Dead blind father of a muted folk who feel their way upward to a life that crushes or absorbs them" (212). Kabnis's discomfort reveals his disrespect. His tortured words barely distinguish him from the "muted folk." Yet Kabnis tries to feel his way up from this underground by coming to terms with his past, with himself, and with his ambition to be a poet.

The impetus for such movement is provided unwittingly by Halsey. The occasion is the basement party Halsey had planned as a kind of orgy with Cora and Stella. However, the guilt Kabnis feels in Father John's presence and in Lewis's apparent moral superiority and racial acceptance dulls his enthusiasm. Lewis accuses Kabnis of trying to escape the past and failing to close the arcs which form the circle of ancestry: "My ancestors were Southern bluebloods" (217), Kabnis whines. Although he feels himself to be in a drama of self-recovery, he participates in it mockingly; he dons a robe, and the speech he utters makes him a "curious spectacle, acting a part, yet very real" (213). Kabnis's mock performance exposes the real torment in his past and his ambitions. He comes to represent all those frustrated men throughout *Cane* whose preference for talk rather than action thwarts any redeeming union with women. Kabnis, like the unnamed speaker in "Avey," ends up being mothered by Cora and Stella rather than possessing them, but his talk reveals the genuine dilemma of self-possession he must resolve: "I've been shapin words after a design that branded here. . . . Been shapin words t fit m soul" (223). Both the language and the speaker are grotesque: "Th form thats burned int my soul is some twisted awful thing that crept in from a dream, a godam nightmare, an wont stay still unless I feed it. An it lives on words. Not beautiful words. God Almighty no. Misshapen, split-gut, tortured, twisted words" (224). Kabnis's language reveals the depth of his descent into the subconscious and the submerged racial heritage.

Kabnis only partially touches base with his art and ancestry. He rightfully understands his artistic calling to be fundamentally different from

Halsey's, who interrupts the silent communication among Father John, Carrie K., and Kabnis by calling him to work. Kabnis also recognizes his brand of intelligence and craft to be more progressive than Halsey's stopped time and obsolete trade: "a soul like mine cant pin itself onto a wagon wheel an satisfy itself in spinnin round. . . . All right for Halsey . . . use him. Me? I get my life down in this scum-hole. Th old man an me" (234–35). Yet Kabnis never fully achieves a unity with his medium as does Halsey, who is "wonderfully himself" in the workshop. Kabnis neither attaches himself fully to the culture of his art nor finds enough meaning in Father John's enigmatic last words (rephrased here as "The sin what's fixed upon the white folks for telling Jesus lies. Oh the sin the white folks committed when they made the Bible lie" [237]) to dispel his feelings of rejection and of being a bastard. Like the grandfather's words in *Invisible Man,* these words haunt Kabnis despite his overly theatrical performance to reclaim his identity underground.

What we do have through Kabnis's descent into racial and artistic consciousness is the surfacing of circular and oracular images to match *Cane*'s spatial and aesthetic design: Kabnis ventures up the stairs from Halsey's cellar at dawn carrying a bucket of dead coals. The morning light behind him illuminates the "soft circle" (239) of Carrie K. kneeling before Father John. A New World artist as messianic figure is *about to be born,* but he hasn't emerged fully from the womb. Toomer thus leaves readers with a freeze-frame of irresolution: the magnetic suspension of arcs of an incomplete circle or of two contradictory, yet complementary scenes held in tableau. Toomer's indeterminacy projects us to the different underworlds of McKay, Wright, and Ellison, and to their various characterizations of the same awakening nation. Kabnis fails to conclude *Cane* because Toomer's material, the culture and landscape of the South, rejects the "swan song" the author imposes upon it. Kabnis's failure to become a "voice of the South" gives others a chance to sing.

One additional singer is Toomer himself. In the long poem "Blue Meridian" (conceived before *Cane* but not published until 1936), Toomer takes a farther step toward the messianic consciousness he had vested in the male characters in *Cane* (recall Dan Moore: "A New World Christ is coming up. Dan comes up" [119]). As the title indicates, the poem depicts the spiritual apex Toomer hoped to achieve for his protagonists and for himself, especially following his initiation into Gurdjieff's philosophy of the universal spiritual harmony among men. "Blue Meridian," as published in *The Wayward and the Seeking,* shows Toomer's spiritual journey going beyond issues of race or nationalism. The poem prophesies "a new America, / To be spiritualized by each new American" (214), and calls into being a unity of man to man:

> Somewhere in our land, in cellars or banks
> In our souls there is a forgotten trust— (219)

Kabnis's venture into a cellar led him to the forgotten trust of ancestry, but *Cane* became too grounded for Toomer, too much of the soil. "Blue Meridian," drawing upon the definition of a meridian as the highest point a heavenly body reaches in its orbit, becomes another way Toomer contemplates the "overarching heavens." The arcs of indeterminancy observed in *Cane* become poles of spiritual consciousness in Toomer's own career, which even today resonates with irresolution and ambiguity (Why did he renounce his blackness? Why did he cease writing prose of publishable quality?).

The "Meridian," beyond and above nationalism or ethnicity, asks the people of European, African, and American Indian origin to build a new race from their separate contributions to America. The poem credits Europeans with growing "towns with the seeds of great cities," the Africans with giving the gift of music, "singing riplets to sorrow in red fields / Sing a swan song, to break rocks," and the great "untamed Navajo" with bringing religion that "Sank into the sacred earth / To fertilize the seven regions of America" (216-17). The poem's omniscient voice, overarching and global, calls forth a new people from these separate groups:

> We are waiting for a new people
> For the joining of men to men
> And man to God. (217)

Out of the union of ethnicity and humanity will come the Universal Man, who will assume a spiritual rather than a racial identity.

Furthermore, the poem argues that men seeking to imbibe the spirituality of the universe

> Must outgrow themselves and their old places
> . . . .
> Must outgrow clan and class, color,

> Nationalism, creed, all the fetishes
> Of the arrested and dismembered,
> And find a larger truth in larger hearts,
> Lest the continents shrink to islands,
> Lest human destiny abort
> And man, bristling against himself, explode. (225)

The poem's speaker was "once an islander," or once a black man; he is now a new American, a universal man, who inhabits a human geography:

> Uncase the nations
> Open this pod by outgrowing it,
> Keep the real but destroy the false;
> We are of the human nation. (226)

The speaker descends from his superior height, and he begins to speak in a familiar, human voice.

Predictably, it is the same Messianic voice readers had heard from the unnamed narrator in "Avey," and from Dan Moore in "Box Seat," who sought to redeem the middle class by his fantasy of destroying its temples (gate front houses and vaudeville theaters) like a New World Samson: "I am going to reach up and grab the girders of this building and pull them down. The crash will be a signal. Hid by the smoke and dust Dan Moore will arise. In his right hand will be a dynamo. In his left, a god's face that will flash white light from ebony" (126).

The same voice speaks as Kabnis, who paraded about underground in his ministerial robes, a "ridiculous pathetic figure" claiming kin with "a family of orators" (222,223) and rejecting Halsey: "Does he think some wooden thing can lift me up?" (234). If *Cane*'s men were incomplete, grounded figures mired in ambivalence brought on by their too literal reading of ancestry, then Toomer's poem will create men of "blue or purple" (232), who will establish a mission for a new savior among the less enlightened:

> My life is given to have
> Realized in our consciousness
> Actualized in life without celebrity,
> This real: wisdom empowered: men growing
> From womb to birth, from birth to rebirth,
> Up arcs of brightness to the resplendent source. (233)

The arcs of a meridian journey to full spirituality merge man with the universe:

> *Blue Meridian, banded-light,*
> *Dynamic atom-aggregate,*
> *Awakes upon the earth;*
> *In his left hand he holds elevated rock,*
> *In his right hand he holds lifted branches,*
> *He dances the dance of the Blue Meridian*
> *And dervishes with the seven regions*
> *of America, and all the world.* (233–34)

The Blue Meridian may be Dan Moore's apotheosis.

Toomer's gesture to wake the nations underground in "Blue Meridian" appears complete: "Lift, lift, thou waking forces! / Let us have the power of man." The impulse to discover ancestry, if not to internalize it, which Toomer initiated in fiction, has progressed to the need to transcend racial identity in the brotherhood the poem creates beyond the boundaries of race and nation. Thus "Blue Meridian" stands in direct contrast to *Cane.* Toomer's indeterminate arcs refer to both texts, one emerging from the soil, the other from the overarching heavens. The arcs representing thematic development actually reveal the dual poles of consciousness in Toomer's career. The poem teaches its author and audience, "Above you will arch a strange universe, / Below you will spread a strange earth" (229). These two places of utterance become a dual magnetic force for Toomer, who explores terrestrial and celestial vistas in order to locate "where the two directions intersect" (233). Toomer's poem extends but does not finally complete his narrative. Whereas *Cane* points to the long journey to self-possession out of the cellar and into the dawn, "Blue Meridian" celebrates "majestic flight" from the soil to the overarching heavens, which brings transcendence within reach. Other writers take up and extend the trajectory of a meridian consciousness. Alice Walker, discussed in Chapter 4, takes Toomer's metaphor of circularity one step farther by changing the spiritual and political ideologies governing the orbit of her protagonist Meridian Hill. Claude McKay shifts the very locus of black achievement away from America and to a larger place of progress in the world.

McKay. From the Ditch to the Bottom: "I will go naked in"

"All my life I have been a troubadour wanderer," concluded Claude McKay in his autobiography, *A Long Way from Home* (1937), "nourishing myself mainly on the poetry of existence." As the close connection between poetry and place here indicates, one of McKay's contributions to Afro-American letters has been his consistent search for a home where art and identity can flourish. His protagonists embark on the same long journey. Jake Brown travels to and from Harlem as a Pullman porter; Ray travels to Marseilles, France, and explores the subterranean life in the slum known as the Ditch; and Bita Plant, who is uprooted from her home in the Bottom, a section of rural Jamaica, for a missionary education in town, then in Britain, returns to blossom in an unexpected embrace of her homeland. McKay's emphasis on place transforms the low life Ditch and the Bottom into places of cultural elevation for his protagonists.

Two sonnets in McKay's "poetry of existence," published during the twenties and reprinted in his *Selected Poems* (1953), show the author's preoccupation with immersion as a way to invert moral values associated with place. By celebrating human instincts, the poet embraces low and high levels of status and exposes the often false distinction between the two. In "Baptism" the speaker sees this movement as private and solitary; he accepts the loneliness of the journey:

> Into the furnace let me go alone;
> Stay you without in terror of the heat.
> I will go naked in—for thus 'tis sweet—
> Into the weird depths of the hottest zone.

The fiery Dantesque descent regenerates the speaker; the purifying flame fortifies him:

> Red aspish tongues shout wordlessly my name.
> Desire destroys, consumes my mortal fears,
> Transforming me into a shape of flame.
> I will come out, back to your world of tears,
> A stronger soul within a finer frame. (35)

Total immersion into experience, into culture, and into self is McKay's remedy for easing the alienation and displacement of outcasts, be they artists or ordinary men and women of color in a white society. If the artistic or racial identity is submerged, hidden, or lost, then a return to instincts and desire would be healing.

A second poem, "Like a Strong Tree," shows instinct to be the hidden resource people have to regain a measure of equilibrium with nature and society.

> Like a strong tree that reaches down deep, deep,
> For sunken water, fluid underground,
> Where the great-ringed unsightly blind worms creep,
> And queer things of the nether world abound:
> So would I live in rich imperial growth,
> Touching the surface and the depth of things,
> Instinctively responsive unto both, (45)

The "sunken water" offers nourishment, and descent into the nether world bears the richest gift: the ability to see and respond to the surface and depth of things. McKay's poetry outlines the terms of his protagonists' confrontation with society and their negotiation between "high" and "low" art, between cultivated literary expression and the ungrammatical but lyrical voice of the folk, represented in McKay's fiction by spontaneous, improvisational music, or jazz.

Home to Harlem introduces McKay's typical protagonist and the author's penchant for picaresque narrative. Ray, a Haitian student working his way through school as a Pullman waiter, meets Jake Brown, a World War I deserter, odd-jobber, and carefree wanderer. Jake befriends Ray and introduces him to common-life situations and people. Ray discovers a brotherhood with fellow Pullman porters and waiters, and he begins to partake of Harlem's nocturnal pleasures, including its "pure voluptuous jazzing" (108). The contrast between Ray and Jake—characters who represent intellect and instinct, or civilization and passionate spontaneity—and the complementary friendship they develop provide a modicum of plot and tension to the novel. Ray gradually identifies with black Americans, sensing in their history of oppression links to the situation in his own country now occupied by American military forces.

Before meeting Jake, however, Ray resented being cast by society into the common lot of blacks whose culture had been driven underground and whose life, in the view of the dominant society, represented nothing more than a negative "underworld":

> The sudden upset of affairs in his home country had landed him into the quivering heart of a naked world whose reality was hitherto unimaginable.

It was what they called in print and polite conversation "the underworld."
The compound word baffled him, as some English words did sometimes.
Why *under*world he could never understand. It was very much upon the
surface as were the other divisions of human life. Having its heights and
middle and depths and secret places even as they. And the people of this
world, waiters, cooks, chauffeurs, sailors, porters, guides, ushers, hod-
carriers, factory hands—all touched in a thousand ways the people of the
other divisions. They worked over there and slept over here, divided by a
street. (224–25)

In the course of the novel Ray learns to enter those depths and secret places
far enough to enjoy life. As Ray is further initiated to Harlem lore, he and
Jake Brown become a pair of opposites, an odd couple. By telling Jake about
Haiti's revolutionary past and some of the grandeur of African history, Ray
imparts a global dimension to the identity and situation of blacks, thus
enlarging Jake's narrow perspective. "As an American Negro [Jake] looked
askew at foreign niggers. Africa was jungle, and Africans bush niggers,
cannibals. And West Indians were monkey-chasers. But now he felt like a
boy who stands with the map of the world in colors before him, and feels the
wonder of the world" (134). And Jake, by initiating Ray into a more carefree
life, brings Ray closer to discovering a way to develop his literary talent.
"Ray had always dreamed of writing words some day. Weaving words to
make romance, ah" (225). Their friendship becomes mutually beneficial.

Yet Ray worries about fulfilling his ambition to be a writer. The literary
models available to him from his education were traditional and European—
works by Dickens, Hugo, Tolstoy, and Chekhov. Ray's intellect pulls him in
one direction, and the sensual vitality in Jake's life pulls him in another. Ray
ponders the surface incompatibility of these two forces. To his "dreams of
making something with words," he muses, "What could he make . . . and
fashion? Could he ever create Art? Art, around which vague, incomprehensible words and phrases stormed?" (228). From the Russian and British
literary masters, Ray learned how "the soil of life saved their roots from the
fire. They were so saturated, so deep-down rooted in it." Faced with the
"utter nakedness and violent coloring of life" Ray has known through Jake,
"Could he create out of the fertile reality around him?" (228). This fertile
reality includes Jake, Zeddy, Strawberry Lips, and a fellow worker suffering
from venereal disease, all of whom the dominant civilization casts into the
"misery of life" where paths to heroism are nearly impossible to perceive and
difficult to follow.

These questions form part of the dilemma Ralph Kabnis faces in *Cane,* and Ray would wallow in a similar static posture of irresolution were it not for McKay's continuous examination of this predicament facing the black writer. The three novels McKay writes to find an answer simply illustrate the gravity of the problem and McKay's unwillingness to settle for easy solutions or ironic distance. In *Home to Harlem* Ray becomes embittered when he realizes his education has left him without guides into a useful artistic life; he rails against the "false feelings that used to be monopolized by educated and cultivated people," and he admonishes another friend, the mulatto James Grant, to educate himself "away from that sort of thing." To make a virtue of "fine feelings" or cultivation, Ray argues, makes people "hollow inside, false and dry as civilization itself." And since civilization is rotten, "we are all rotten who are touched by it" (242–43). Ray, reeling from being rejected by the dominant civilization, finds new values in the under-world life where he questions received values and spatial associations. His argument sounds more final than it really is: "I have seen your high and mighty civilized people do things that some pimps would be ashamed of.... Do it in the name of civilization.... And I have been forced down to the level of pimps and found some of them more than human" (244). To illustrate his point Ray tells a story, which is the whole of the subsequent chapter titled "He Also Loved." It is a tale of eternal love between a prostitute and her pimp, who commits suicide following the woman's fatal illness. The tale expresses art and human value as well as Ray's nascent talent as a storyteller. He begins to embrace the soil of black life in America and disregards the dominant culture's limited view of what constitutes appropriate material for literature. This moment of storytelling is Ray's performance in the "underworld."

Yet *Home to Harlem* never resolves Ray's dilemma. McKay ends the novel with Ray leaving on a freighter bound for Europe. In the geographical home of the dominant culture, Ray feels more like "a slave of civilized tradition" (263). Jake remains a model of the way blacks can live full lives in the "melancholy-comic" environment of Harlem where "voluptuous jazzing" or "the mad, contagious music and high laughter" animates everyone. The music, of course, is the blues, which Ray remembers coming from another underground place, "a Harlem basement before dawn" (266), a setting similar to Halsey's cellar at the close of *Cane.* The memorable tones in this melancholy-comic music and the vitality of Harlem accompany Ray in his travels. His journey links Afro-American identity to the fate of African peoples in the modern world where interpretations of what is primitive or civilized restrict black progress and justify racial oppression.

In McKay's second novel *Banjo,* Ray's bitterness towards civilization turns to hatred. After vagabonding throughout Europe, Ray settles temporarily in Marseilles, France, where he faces his dilemma head on. In the Quartier Réservé near the docks, known among beachcombers as The Ditch, he meets Lincoln Agrippa Daily, who is known as Banjo for the instrument he plays. The novel, subtitled "A Story Without a Plot," recounts the picaresque adventures Ray and Banjo share with displaced blacks from Africa, the Caribbean, Europe, and America. Through these adventures Ray touches base with the culture-nourishing ancestry and art. Reviewing *Banjo* in *Crisis* magazine, Du Bois praised the novel for presenting something of an "international philosophy of the Negro race" (234). That philosophy emerges from McKay's verbal geography of Marseilles, which endows lowly Bum Square, Boody Lane, and other corners of the Ditch with values important in elevating Ray to fulfill his literary aspirations. He becomes a writer and a reader of various black cultures in flux due to displacement or forced immigration to Europe. Several documents mentioned in the novel suggest the range of ideas contained within this "philosophy" of racial uplift as well as chart Ray's progress to solidarity with blacks suffering worldwide oppression. What sustains them all is the culture they share from mother Africa. McKay's references to Pan-African journals and publications of the twenties point away from the "race problem" in the United States and merge displaced blacks into a brotherhood. *La Race Nègre,* Marcus Garvey's *Negro World,* and the controversial anticolonialist novel *Batouala,* winner of the prestigious Prix Goncourt in 1921, document Ray's intellectual journey and foreshadow the impact of the literary movement of Négritude in the thirties. Although Ray repeats in *Banjo* the same kind of episodic events as in *Home to Harlem,* these documents represent a key difference between the two novels as well as a progression in McKay's thinking. *Banjo*'s importance thus extends beyond the conventions and landscape of the picaresque novel. It becomes McKay's critique of the cultural misdirection of the Harlem Renaissance, which favored portrayals of bourgeois respectability and assimilation, and becomes a harbinger of the literary movement that celebrates the multiple forms of black art. For Négritude, like Ray, attempts to redeem and reclaim African identity from the arbitrary lower levels of cultural inferiority to which it has been consigned in both Europe and America. Ray comes to discover the source of his literature and a celebration of racial consciousness in the spontaneous verbal and musical art the vagabonds create continuously.

The vagabonds and their leader Banjo avenge their common rejection by Europe by beachcombing, panhandling, and roughhousing in the city known as "Europe's best back door" (69), which is geographically symbolic because Marseilles sits squarely between Europe and Africa. For these estranged sons seeking kin, Marseilles's port of call offers an exchange of cultural values and a chance to discover hidden racial attributes: "In no other port had [Ray] seen congregated such a picturesque variety of Negroes. Negroes speaking the civilized tongues, Negroes speaking all the African dialects, black Negroes, brown Negroes, yellow Negroes. It was as if every country of the world where Negroes lived had sent representatives drifting in to Marseilles. A great vagabond host of jungle-like Negroes trying to scrape a temporary existence from the macadamized surface of this great Provençal port" (68). Affirming new values, particularly self-respect, and the art of storytelling and music, the vagabonds create humane, supportive bonds among themselves to oppose the divide-and-conquer strategy the West usually instigates among the people it subjugates.

The spontaneity of the storytelling and music-playing events proves the existence of a common base for black art. The various types of performance the vagabonds elicit from each other manifest group membership and solidarity. The improvised storytelling Ray participates in establishes African folklore as a common source for many New World black literatures. Likewise, the orchestra Banjo wants to create becomes a symphony of disparate instruments and voices when the men gather to play blues and jazz numbers such as "Stay Carolina Stay" (a version of "Jelly Roll Blues" [46]) and "Shake That Thing." The music and the folktales transmit common denominators in African cultures. The art reflects the residual "international" Africanist philosophy emerging from the core friendship between Ray and Banjo.

Ray's complementarity with Banjo, more than with Jake, combines the literary arts with music. Banjo, who calls Ray "a writing black" and a "book fellah," appreciates Ray's artistic talent. Jake is impressed with the mere fact that Ray has had an education ("Ef I was edjucated, I could understand things better and be proper-speaking like you is" [*Home to Harlem,* 273]). And Banjo affirms the direct stake he has in the submerged culture. His banjo is doubly instrumental; it is a source of identity, and it makes music. In Banjo's words, it is "moh than a gal, moh than a pal, it's mah-self" (6).

When Ray's envy of Banjo's independence surfaces in the words "You've got your banjo to work for you," Banjo retorts, "And youse got you' pen" (149), which reminds Ray of his similar responsibility. From his artistic complementarity with Banjo, Ray learns to value self-expression and performance in music, storytelling, and dance, which encourage him to seek an audience for the "poetry of existence" he writes.

In addition to developing an artistic complementarity, the two main characters share their different geographical sensibilities. Ray, a French-speaking Haitian, shows Banjo a side of Marseilles he hadn't known before. "Ray suggested taking a turn along the Corniche. Banjo had never been on the Corniche. . . . [Ray] liked the Corniche in a special way, when he was in one of those oft-recurring solitary, idly-brooding moods" (69). And Banjo, a southern black American, shows Ray places in the Ditch he had never known to exist: "Banjo had the freedom of the Ditch and, as his pal, Ray shared some of it and was introduced to the real depths of the greater Ditch beyond his alley at the extreme end" (93). The characters reveal to each other the inner and outer geography of Marseilles, its physical and metaphorical landscape. Together, Banjo and Ray find the best places to perform their art. Europe's "best back door" becomes a stage for enacting the larger drama of cultural revalidation. However, before Ray can fully reject bourgeois elitism, which relegates the blues and folklore beneath the ken of sophisticated or redemptive art, he must descend through the multiple levels of culture in the submerged nation Banjo unveils. Kinship, especially for alienated artists of the African diaspora, must be earned.

The life Ray embraces in the Ditch increases his alienation from Europe. Rather than contain his bitterness, Ray preaches against civilization and its false promise of social advancement. The real route to an authentic artistic renaissance, Ray believes, lies elsewhere: "You get a white man's education and learn to despise your own people," Ray argues. "If this renaissance we're talking about is going to be more than a sporadic and scabby thing, we'll have to get down to our racial roots to create it" (200). Ray concludes his argument by following his instincts for cultural affirmation: "Only when he got down among the black and brown working boys and girls of the country did he find something of that raw unconscious and the-devil-with-them pride in being Negro that was his own natural birthright. Down there the ideal skin was brown skin" (320). Furthermore, Ray acts upon the manifesto of cultural autonomy he voiced earlier in the novel. " 'The best Negroes are *not* the society Negroes. I am not writing for them, nor the poke-chop-abstaining Negroes, nor the Puritan Friends of Color, nor the Negrophobes nor the Negrophiles. I am writing for people who can stand a real story no matter where it comes from' " (117). From the lowest "ditch" of existence Ray delivers the same message Langston Hughes had announced from the racial mountaintop. Writing in the *Nation,* Hughes asserted: "We younger Negro artists who create now intend to express our individual dark-skinned selves without fear or shame. If white people are pleased we are glad. If they are not, it doesn't matter. We know we are beautiful. And ugly too. The tom-tom cries and the tom-tom laughs. If colored people are pleased we are glad. If they are not, their displeasure doesn't matter either. We build our temples for tomorrow, strong as we know how, and we stand on top of the mountain, free within ourselves." McKay's path to that mountaintop of self-possession goes along the lower frequencies of the Ditch. " 'The wul' goes round and round,' " Banjo says, adding a geometrical shape to his reckoning with time and space. " 'And I keeps right on gwine around with it' " (304).

Thus in *Banjo* Ray rejects civilization as vehemently as he feels rejected by it. The extremity of this position leads to a self-righteous tone in Ray's proclamation, which is compromised by Ray's lack of productivity. McKay backs himself into such a corner that he all but extinguishes any hope that intellect and instinct, education and passion, can coexist for black writers as they have for Russian novelists like Tolstoy, whose art, Ray believes, grew from the soil. The quest McKay began with Ray meeting Jake on a moving train—an overground railroad—and continued until Ray's ultimate break with civilization and embrace of vagabonding finds a more balanced conclusion in *Banana Bottom.* In the earlier novels McKay attempted to survey the wilderness of black alienation and displacement. In his last novel, McKay finds peace with himself through his female protagonist Bita Plant who, uprooted from Jamaica and grafted with a European education, manages to transplant herself back in the native soil.

McKay's choice of a female protagonist to complete his quest shows his desire for regeneration. Bita fulfills the potential of McKay's bachelor wanderers. Her procreative union with her peasant husband Jubban, in which both are "nourished by the same soil," resolves McKay's dilemma of unification with land, culture, and self. McKay previously depicted divided sensibilities through oppositional friendships between men, which limit creativity to the realm of art. This is not to say that Jake and Banjo fail as mates for Ray, but that the union goes only so far. Through the "offspring" of literature Ray represents his racial ambivalence or displacement. And Ray does locate Harlem and the Ditch as places for the performance of his identity. Bita Plant, however, embodies regeneration.

By returning in *Banana Bottom* to the time and place of his West Indian upbringing, McKay frees himself from the overwhelming cultural tradition of Europe and from American myths of racial uplift through face-saving art (a dominant ideology during the Harlem Renaissance). McKay is also free to explore the range of characters, situations, and life opportunities a predominantly black environment provides. Readers encounter a similar ease in Zora Neale Hurston's fiction, which takes place in the all-black town of Eatonville, Florida. McKay and Hurston luxuriate in lavish descriptions of quotidian events, customs, and the various features of the land. Yet McKay worried about the possibility of exaggeration and imprecision in his writing. He once commented disparagingly in a letter to his longtime friend Max Eastman, "Whether poetry or prose, my writing is always most striking and true when it is a little reminiscent and nostalgic. The vividness of *Home to Harlem* was due to my being removed just the right distance from the scene. Doing *Banjo* I was too close to it. *Banana Bottom* was a lazy dream, the images becoming blurred from overdoing long-distance photography" (211). The imagery, no matter how imprecise, clearly helped McKay resolve some long-standing, as well as long-distance, conflicts, for the novel celebrates Bita's successful reintegration into her home society.

Tabitha Plant, nicknamed Bita, is raped by a crazed neighbor before she has reached puberty. She is "adopted" by an English missionary couple in the larger town of Jubilee, where she is raised in the church. To complete her education, Bita is later sent to England. On her return to Jubilee, she becomes dissatisfied with the sterile life at the mission and prefers the rural life in her birthplace Banana Bottom. She also rejects the suitors her adoptive parents have selected. Once her own father dies, Bita is free to marry the man of her choice, Jubban, her father's farmhand, and to embrace rural life. The missionaries, Malcolm and Priscilla Craig, actually wanted to turn Bita into an experiment. Their attempt to uproot Bita from the nurturing soil of homeland results in her more fervent attachment to it. Bita doesn't reject her education, she simply refuses to be alienated from her past and from her country. Bita rejects roles imposed upon her by a racist and sexist "civilization" that values the hybrid blossom rather than the sustaining roots. Like Zora Neale Hurston's protagonist, Janie Starks, Bita rejects the comfort of her life with the Craigs and the predictable "automation" of her rise in society. She also rejects the lesser-educated but lighter-skinned "elite" of the island. One suitor, Herald Newton Day, approved by the Craigs because he has trained for the ministry and will succeed them at the mission, shares Bita's kind of education. But Day has so absorbed conservative thinking that he reminds Bita of her limited opportunities as a dark-complexioned woman, which he reinforces rather than rejects in his effort to become the spiritual leader of the community. The perversity in his blind ambition and subtle exploitation of Bita's race, color, and gender soon becomes apparent. Day represents a false hope; his kind of new day never materializes. When he is caught fornicating with a goat, he disgraces the town and his family. As for Bita, an even better day is dawning.

Bita looks beyond the superficial trappings of civilization that had disguised Day's perversity and insanity all along. Her personality and learning nurture deeper roots, for Bita refuses to graft onto Banana Bottom those conventional designations of low and high levels of sophistication. Like Ray among the Pullman porters in America or with the vagabond musicians in France, Bita finds the highest cultural and spiritual values in the honest life in Banana Bottom where the hilly geography defies its name and reveals its high moral value. Bita attends the tea-meetings full of dancing, music, and "bad company," and there discovers the satisfying customs that give vitality and purpose to her life.

The stage is set for Bita's development from the time she is deflowered by Crazy Bow, the village fiddler who rapes her. Like Banjo, Crazy Bow is instrumental in Bita's life, for his deed sets in motion McKay's familiar conflict between primitivism and civilization. As a musician, Crazy Bow embodies the melancholy-comic dualism McKay had always recognized as the redemptive feature of black music. The rape ironically makes it possible for Bita to confront civilization and to reckon in different terms with the opportunities available to black women. Crazy Bow "knew all kinds of music: village tunes, hymns and anthems, jubilee songs, and snatches of high music" (6). When he succumbs to Bita's childish, playful wrestling, which ends in her rape, he unwittingly forces Bita to create new ways of regaining wholeness and integrity, and of blossoming into her own.

The Craigs' offer to educate Bita provides but one way out of the despair of rape. Their plan, however, ends up making Bita more of an automaton than a well-rounded person: "You have received an education," Priscilla Craig reminds Bita, "to make you see and do the correct thing almost automatically" (45). The Craigs' goal for Bita is artificial and alienating.

Bita comes close to resembling Ralph Kabnis, whose false claim to southern "blue blood" ancestry exposes his artificiality: "He totters as a man would who for the first time uses artificial limbs. As a completely artificial man would" (*Cane,* 163). Luckily, Bita's instinctive love for the people saves her from the doomed fate of Kabnis and of Herald Newton Day.

Bita also finds a refuge in her friendship with Squire Gensir, a "mentor" character like Banjo and Jake. But Gensir is white, and he functions as a bridge between Bita's cultural past and her present educational achievement. An amateur collector of island folksongs and lore, Gensir convinces Bita of the natural pleasure of tea-meetings and encourages her to discover the cultural wealth of Banana Bottom: "Your folklore is the spiritual link between you and your ancestral origin" (125). Dancing at these occasions and enjoying the music, Bita manifests her identity in these performances of racial belonging. She dances "down the barrier between high breeding and common pleasures" (84). Thus Bita enriches the community as much as the community enriches her. By mingling with crowds early on in her return home, she comes to experience McKay's own metaphor of baptism, entering the "weird depths of the hottest zone." At a marketplace, Bita responds to the sights, smells, and touch of crowds. "It gave her the sensation of a reservoir of familiar kindred humanity into which she had descended for baptism" (40). Bita's homecoming, unlike Ray's cerebral sojourn in the Ditch, engages all her senses.

Bita engineers her descent into the well of humanity and her corresponding ascent to identity by refusing to accept received notions of black inferiority or despair. She gives new significance to McKay's title of *Banana Bottom* through her own discovery and articulation of the elevated spiritual value the submerged nation had possessed all along. Bita's progress from being a country "wildling" to the mature wife of Jubban brings both characters back to the love they share for the soil as well as for each other. Their complementarity is regenerative: "Her music, her reading, her thinking were the flowers of her intelligence and he the root in the earth upon which she was grafted, both nourished by the same soil" (313). This is the home and the nation Claude McKay acknowledges finally as his own.

CHAPTER THREE

Trouble about my grave: Richard Wright, Ralph Ellison, and LeRoi Jones

Toomer's journey to the South and McKay's long search abroad for links with the African diaspora led their protagonists into "holes," "ditches," or "bottoms" as places of cultural elevation. Later experiments by Wright, Ellison, and Jones examine how protagonists perform particular acts of cultural belonging or alienation on similar underground stages, away from the scrutiny of whites or the censure of blacks. Unlike the ever-changing landscape for wandering troubadours depicted by McKay (the musician Banjo) and Toomer ("Caroling softly souls of slavery"), Wright, Ellison, and Jones explore a stationary, male-dominated subterranean world. It is an arena where fugitives, criminals, displaced leftists, and "black Baudelaires" reenact their initial alienation from the world to perform ritual acts of reintegration.

These writers use various figurations of the lower depths or "lower frequencies" to connect with myths (Jones's play *Dutchman* is set in the *"flying underbelly"* of the city, *"heaped in modern myth"* [3]). Their "descent" parallels the directions taken by Zora Neale Hurston, Alice Walker, and Gayl Jones to reach "womanist" landscapes where porches, petunias, and even prisons help them to reconstruct myths. (Walker's essay "In Search of Our Mothers' Gardens" gives direction to the road imagery in Hurston's fiction and reinvents the woman's role as nurturer. Gayl Jones offers imagery counter to the Edenic pastoral and to northbound freedom journeys in her sardonic portrait of Eva Medina Canada in *Eva's Man.*) Each group of writers expands the parameters of cultural mobility previously restricted by gender, race, sexual exploitation, or the artistic struggle to create meaning out of chaos, which may be simply another word for wilderness.

The sewer, cellar, or subway settings in the fictions of Wright, Ellison, and Jones have offered two stark and disturbing options: a cradle for the rebirth of the hero, or a roaring, watery grave at his death. The underground is either a nourishing womb or a troublesome, bitter grave. One difference between the men and the women writers mentioned here lies in the various ways their protagonists reinvent self through verbal performances in alternative landscapes. Even when a character surfaces from underground and finds refuge in a house that appears to offer some domestic tranquility, he or she must beware of the prison that may lurk underneath the porches or beyond the allure of petunias.

Richard Wright. "The Landless upon the land"

Wright's poem "Between the World and Me" (1935) strengthened his debut as a writer and introduced him to a literal wilderness that yielded a theme potent enough to preoccupy him throughout his career: the poet's alienation from the world around him. Entering the woods, the speaker chances upon the charred remains of a tree and a lynched black man. The details of this grisly death transport him back into the time and space of the event. He assumes the voice of the victim, indeed becomes the victim. The ground grips the passive speaker as "the sooty details of the scene rose, thrusting / themselves between the world and me. . . . " Some details indicate the event was mere entertainment for whites: "butt-ends of cigars and cigarettes, peanut shells, a drained gin-flask" (246). Other evidence partially resurrects the human object of their fun: "A vacant shoe, an empty tie, a ripped shirt, a lonely hat, and a pair of trousers stiff with black blood" (246). The speaker is so overwhelmed by the mounting evidence that when the next casual stroller enters the woods, the speaker is now the "dry bones," *his* face "a stony skull staring in yellow surprise at the sun" (247). The woods, an appropriate setting for death and transformation, is the place where the writer assumes voice and subject. The career Wright embarks upon will depict other barriers, or Du Boisian "veils," between him and the world. In *American Hunger* (posthumously published in 1977), Wright endeavored to bridge such gaps and to ease the invisibility imposed upon him: "I wanted to try to build a bridge of words between me and that world outside" (135).

Situating this poem in Wright's career helps us to understand how his voice emerges from a reaction to racial violence as well as from "the ethics" of surviving de facto segregation. This is the bifocal lens through which Wright viewed the world. His characters necessarily are marginal men and women, criminals, and sharecroppers trapped in the narrow orbit of racial etiquette and economic displacement; all are among the "landless upon the land" (165). It is no accident that Wright would stake his emergence as a writer upon his escape from the social status and "place" prescribed for him. Like the fugitives during slavery, Wright headed to the North. His search for a literary voice, however, drew him back to the land that had alienated him; his song in a strange land required exile and return. The imaginative geography in his fiction reflects not only what he called his "self-achieved literacy," but also his self-created space. In *American Hunger,* Wright argues that the notion of self-achieved literacy fueled his break with the American Communist party, which deemed self-advancement as too threatening: "Even a Negro, entrapped by ignorance and exploitation—as I had been—could, if he had the will and love for it, learn to read and understand the world in which he lived. And it was these people that the Communists could not understand" (120).

If the poems Wright published in the journals *Left Front, New Masses,* and *Partisan Review* launched his career, then the short fiction and nonfictional prose helped to secure it. His reliance on melodrama and naturalism put him on the defensive, particularly when he confronted the work of another black writer, a veteran of the Harlem Renaissance, who was telling a different story from the same southern landscape. One year after Wright published his much anthologized story, "Big Boy Leaves Home," and just before the volume *Uncle Tom's Children* appeared in print, Zora Neale Hurston published *Their Eyes Were Watching God.* Her view of the South as a land rich in folklore, full of a zest for life and adventure, as seen through the lives of Janie Starks and Tea Cake Vergible Woods, directly challenged Wright's more ideological view that this environment was debilitating enough to require his escape, violent enough to merit his hostility. Wright's response to Hurston's novel was his negative review published in *New Masses* (October 5, 1937), revealing their conflicting claims to the same territory: "Her characters eat and laugh and work and kill; they swing like a pendulum in that safe and narrow orbit in which America likes to see the Negro live: between laughter and tears." These dismissive words should remind us of James Weldon Johnson's critique of Paul Laurence Dunbar's dialect poems for the same reasons; they were too confined to the "two full stops [of] humor and pathos" (41). That an anxiety of literary influence and heritage (as suggested by Harold Bloom) may have motivated Johnson's remarks can be seen in his early derivative poem, "Sence You Went Away," written in the Dunbaresque dialect he found so objectionable. Similarly, Wright tried to clear a space for himself away from Hurston's lively terrain. He would leave the South, which, to his dismay (in "How Bigger Was Born") "even bankers' daughters could read and weep over and feel good about" (xxvii). Wright then claimed the squalor and violence of the northern ghetto through Bigger Thomas in *Native Son,* in which "native" establishes both Wright's and Bigger's identity in geographical terms. Yet Hurston was not the only challenge to Wright's coveted ideological stance. Other key figures who inhabited the landscape Wright wanted to master included his real Uncle Tom, his grandmother, and his father. Wright's fiction, until the achievement of his autobiography, narrates his subjective assessment of the "narrowness" of that familial, regional, and cultural orbit.

These family members were not only guardians of Wright's childhood, but they also dominated much of the space in which he matured. Wright wrested control from them by emigrating out of the orbit of their influence in the Jim Crow South and by negatively depicting their ties to the land. This same land, paradoxically, remains the source of his imprisonment and the means of his freedom: by reimagining the South in his writing and characterizing members of his family, even disparagingly, Wright gains authority over the past and over the confining physical environment of the South, the place of his past. If control of the past helps to determine the future, then Wright would shape how readers will see him. He took hold of the language and the literature his grandmother had denied him in her religious prohibition against books as "lies." He also gave himself a heroism of escape, uplift, and rebirth through deliverance, as in a slave narrative (Wright was born on a sharecropping plantation in Mississippi), by structuring his autobiography to replace the self in literary history and redesign the physical space of the past. Wright's fiction, from *Uncle Tom's Children* to *Native Son* to "The Man Who Lived Underground," testifies to his use of language as a way of measuring his distance from the past, yet reveals how unwittingly Wright was as much within as without the orbit he thought too narrow to contain, educate, discipline, or finally restrict him. These works suggest Wright's developing need for autobiography as an art of the self, even a fictionalized self. His formal control of language and experience also led him to construct an imaginary haven for that new self. Two years after the completion of *Black Boy* (1945), Wright left the United States for

France. His expatriation reflected the ultimate act of ownership: only a native son can disown a native land. A better understanding of this movement in Wright's fiction as well as his invention of spaces for refuge and regeneration is provided by examining those key scenes in his work, especially "The Man Who Lived Underground," that shape his long and often tortuous attempt to locate self and home in the "wider" orbit of his prose.

Wright's first book, *Uncle Tom's Children,* opens with a story about departure. "Big Boy Leaves Home" also details the consequences of the accidental killing of a white man who had intruded upon the playful swim of several black boys. The guilty Big Boy escapes mob violence only by securing refuge in a hillside kiln where he witnesses the lynching of his innocent friend Bobo. The placement of this story in the volume and in Wright's canon is important because it introduces his most persistent theme and fixes the sequence of events and geographical metaphors that will reappear in successive works: fugitive escape from society and into hiding that offers either rebirth or a probable grave, which is Wright's image of black life. The story that closes the collection in its first edition, "Fire and Cloud," is superseded in later editions by a hint of spatial optimism in "Bright and Morning Star," suggesting a height to which the protagonists might aspire. Witnessing Bobo's lynching informs Big Boy of the fate that awaits him should he leave the hard-earned refuge of the kiln prematurely (he has killed a snake to gain entry and strangled a dog that discovered his hideout; these ritual slayings earn him refuge, then rebirth when he finally escapes to the North). Wright's metaphor of the star suggests a higher consciousness guiding Big Boy as well as Wright's readers.

Naming the collection *Uncle Tom's Children* satirizes the proverbial black man contented with his place in society. In view of Wright's developing autobiography, the title also identifies a real uncle named Tom, whom Wright has to fight to get free of the restrictions of Jim Crow ethics and to plan his "leaving home." In *Black Boy,* young Wright, armed with razors, fights back when Uncle Tom tries to discipline him. The emotional stress evoked in the scene and its turning point in Wright's life recall Frederick Douglass's fight with slavebreaker Covey. Both authors recognize this fight as pivotal. After breaking the slavebreaker, Douglass changes from thinking, feeling, and acting like a slave to planning his escape and acquiring freedom:

> This battle with Mr. Covey was the turning-point in my career as a slave.
> It rekindled the few expiring embers of freedom, and revived within me a

sense of my own manhood. It recalled the departed self-confidence, and inspired me again with a determination to be free. . . . I felt as I never felt before. It was a glorious resurrection, from the tomb of slavery, to the heaven of freedom. My long-crushed spirit rose, cowardice departed, bold defiance took its place; and I now resolved that, however long I might remain a slave in form, the day had passed forever when I could be a slave in fact. (*Narrative,* 104-5)

Similarly, when Wright's Uncle Tom backs away from him, saying, "Somebody will yet break your spirit," Wright immediately sees him not as an example, but a "warning" (140). Wright later reflected: "Though I must have seemed brutal and desperate to him, I had never thought of myself as being so, and now I was appalled at how I was regarded. It was a flash of insight which revealed to me the true nature of my relations with my family, an insight which altered the entire course of my life. I was now definitely decided upon leaving home" (*Black Boy,* 152). These fight scenes in both narratives are important rituals in each writer's search for a more autonomous identity. Douglass's fight on the plantation threshing floor and Wright's disruption of his household by fire (recall his arson when a child) and force prefigure a triumph over spaces of confinement that breed obsequious behavior.

Beyond filial confrontation, however, Wright has set up a paradigm for the way his protagonists, other children of Uncle Tom, will wrest their identities from specific persons or places. This movement within the self and within the physical and cultural landscape is not without risks. "The Man Who Lived Underground" (1944) describes both the physical and psychological gambles Fred Daniels takes when he is falsely accused of a crime and beaten by the police. He escapes from them and finds refuge in the city sewer, which becomes an alternative space underground where he can establish and act upon an identity different from what black as well as white society imposed upon him. Daniels's initial descent, like Big Boy's retreat to the kiln, is restorative, but the urban den for Daniels shows how few options may await a Big Boy upon his reaching the North. As Wright puts it in *12 Million Black Voices,* the landless escape domination by the rural Lords of the Land only to be suppressed by urban Bosses of Buildings. Douglass and other fugitive slaves felt a similar frustration upon finding the North only slightly less threatening and restrictive than the South. Indeed, implicit in Wright's naming his protagonist Daniels may be his ironic reply to the query raised in one optimistic slave song:

Didn't my Lord deliver Daniel
Then why not everyman?

In the lion's den of the urban slum and sewer (signs of deterioration and waste), Wright envisions Daniels as a different everyman—one more like himself, whom the Lord neither redeemed nor delivered. Wright's as yet unpublished essay "Memories of My Grandmother" reveals how central this story is as a textual bridge between *Native Son* and *Black Boy,* and as a high point in Wright's conquest of his past: "The whole idea back of the novel is centered around the ardent and volatile religious disposition of my grandmother who died in Chicago in 1934" (1, hereafter cited as *MOMG*).

As Wright's invisible man, Daniels mediates between the demands of autobiography and fiction, between the temptation of exile and the pain of return to familial, ancestral territory. Wright himself admitted to feeling more exhilarated and satisfied writing "The Man Who Lived Underground" than any other fiction in his still burgeoning career: "I have never written anything in my life that stemmed more from sheer inspiration, or executed any piece of writing in a deeper feeling of imaginative freedom, or expressed myself in a way that followed more naturally from my own personal background, reading, experiences, and feelings than 'The Man Who Lived Underground.' In fact, I can say that, in the act of writing, for the first time in my life, I reacted as a *whole* to the material before me in an effort to create a simple, yielding surface of prose" (*MOMG,* 1).

The genesis of the novella and its composition reveal much about Wright's search for place in fiction and in autobiography. Wright situated himself in both genres as a way of coming to terms with a restrictive, debilitating past, dominated by poles of emotions represented in the family by his vengeful grandmother and uncle and loving, but sickly mother, and in the outside world by the competing ideologies of religion and communism. Wright's mother, Ella, was the only one who encouraged his imagination to fly, to soar, to break the bonds of his repressive home and society. Exploring these themes in the nearly surrealistic posture of Fred Daniels, Wright progressed to a point of being able to write his own story, just as Daniels in the secrecy of an underground cave performs an act of nascent storytelling by typing the beginning of his tale. Wright's emergence as a writer, which appears complete when *Black Boy* and *American Hunger* are read as one volume, is dramatized allegorically and autobiographically in "The Man Who Lived Underground." The joy of release Wright felt in creating Daniels's character must have propelled him into composing *Black Boy,* wherein the author could at last become his own protagonist, substituting an action for Daniels's literary gesture of typing the novella's opening line (in an earlier draft, according to Michel Fabre), "It was a long hot day." The action in the opening chapter of *Black Boy* is young Wright setting fire to the house dominated by his ailing grandmother. It is also, paradoxically, the same house under which the child took refuge, desiring to be unseen: "I yearned to become invisible, to stop living" (5).

Wright's first lesson about invisibility as a source for the novella came from the grandmother, Margaret Bolden Wilson, whose strict adherence to Seventh Day Adventist doctrine required that she and her family live *in* the world but avoid being *of* the world. The emotional and intellectual detachment Wright felt in her personality made her home a prison; her religiously justified alienation was a measure of her willful invisibility. A creative and punitive matron, she imposed her own version of biblical lore: "she took concepts from the Old Testament and tagged the items in her environment which did not fit and gave them other names and other meanings." Yet Wright detected a defiant spirit in his grandmother, which became inspiration of a different kind. She was a rebel "militantly at war with every particle of reality she saw." He describes her more vividly as having "deep-set black eyes with overhanging lids and she had a habit of gazing with a steady, unblinking stare; in my later life I've always associated her religious ardor with those never-blinking eyes of hers, eyes that seemed to be *in* this world but not *of* this world, eyes that seemed to be contemplating human frailty from some invulnerable position outside time and space. . . . Always she seemed to be peeping out of Heaven into the world while living in the world" (*MOMG,* 8–9).

What helped Granny, in Wright's view, to maintain her moral superiority was her unshakable faith in the invisible presence of God in the world, another point against which Wright measured himself: "The idea of invisibility dates back in my life to the religious teachings of my childhood, for my grandmother's entire attitude toward life was based on 'the substance of things hoped for, and the evidence of things unseen.' " Wright preferred concrete engagement with the world, the touch and feel of real life. Yet "my hostility toward my grandmother's religion did not keep its influence from registering upon my sensibilities during my adolescence" (*MOMG,* 14). Although his "religious grandmother's interpretation of life" made him leave home at fifteen, Wright would recreate her ambivalence toward the world by making

Fred Daniels an invisible man: "It is but natural that I should have become excited over the question of how it would feel to stand outside of life and look at life" (*MOMG,* 15).

When he came to write the novella, Wright sought to capture "the inner structure of my grandmother's religion." He searched for a suitable form. "I do not mean literary form, but form of action, a contour of movement, a ritualistic scheme whose dynamics would lay bare the inner but not the outer processes of religion" (*MOMG,* 3). Whereas Wright casts a religious temperament in a secular mold, James Baldwin, as shown in Chapter 5, uses "the outer processes of religion" to project a secular, indeed "profane" sensibility. An article in *Detective* magazine about an underground burglar in Hollywood, nicknamed "the Mole," gave Wright just the source he needed for the outer story: a man who plans and executes his crimes unseen. Wright thus combined the outer realistic story with an inner ritualistic action to manifest his grandmother's religion and to shape his rebellion from it. For Wright, the underground became a place to gather up the fragments of an abusive family life and a vantage point from which he could participate in the real world, however racist it was. The sewer, for Wright, was the best place for this kind of "improvisation": Daniels's "crawling around sewers . . . might be linked to anyone's sense of groping through the days of one's life," admits Wright as he navigates those murky waters for better control over the years of his life.

In "The Man Who Lived Underground," Wright transforms invisibility from a self-effacing and alienating flaw into a precondition for self-creation. An earlier version of the manuscript has Daniels feeling compassion for the police who falsely arrested him and necessitated his escape into the sewer: "He wanted to go to them and tell them they were wasting their time; that even if they found him it was not worth the effort that they were expending. Not that he had a desire to give himself up. No! He wanted to help the policeman and at the same time be quite safe, just as he was now: *in* the world but somehow *out* of it, *looking* at it but *free* of it" (ms., 94). The longer Daniels stays underground, the greater is his separation from the values of the aboveground world, and more important, the freer Wright becomes from the repression and restrictions of his grandmother. Wright has Daniels command a radio, meat cleaver, and a typewriter, objects that Granny would not allow in the house: "She ordered me to destroy the first radio I brought into the house. She refused to believe that the music and the voices were coming over the air; she branded it an evil thing of the devil"

(*MOMG,* 11). Daniels eats to his heart's content, whereas the Wright of *Black Boy* is always hungry, which suggests a reason for the earlier title of the autobiography to evoke multiple forms of deprivation, *American Hunger.* Daniels also has more money than he knows what to do with. Granny valued money to relieve the family's poverty; money also tempered Granny's hostility toward Wright the one time he was the sole family breadwinner. Underground, Daniels alters the utility of money and breaks free of the controlling influence of family (he forgets all about his wife) and transcends societal restrictions. He emerges from the underground a different man, beyond the authority of home, church, and state (the singing congregation and the brutal police officers, Lawson and Murphy, who had forced a murder confession from him, thus setting his escape in motion). Upon discovering in the underground cave that he can give new meaning to objects and new significance to the subterranean space, he embraces a new, self-chosen identity. Daniels is no longer a fugitive, but someone armed with sensitivity, perhaps even a higher intelligence, which renders him more vulnerable than before:

> Fred Daniels's roused and tense sensibilities registered everything he saw in terms of a man about to make a decision. The decision he did make was determined by what he could *take for granted.* He went directly to the police who had branded him guilty when he had seen his fill in the underground. Where else was there for him to go? The police had given him his meaningful life, such as it was, filled with horror. This is not surprising; my grandmother was a stickler for obeying all the laws she hated and condemned. . . . The criminal who returns, in spite of himself, to the scene of his crime, the murderer, full of remorse, who goes to the police, is performing more than an overt act. He is *completing* a logical circle of feeling over which he, within the limits in which he lives, has no control. Man does not and cannot live alone, and if he tries to, he ceases to be a man. (*MOMG,* 47)

Wright wants to show this vulnerability to be the source of Daniels's humanity. Moreover, knowledge, however stolen, becomes the proof of his humanness, as it was for Frederick Douglass. As a fully realized "human" character Daniels must now confront an irony of life: the inevitability of death. "In the actual process of writing I found that I could make the whole theme of stolen knowledge ironical by having Fred Daniels discover a knowledge," Wright admits, "whose utmost value he would not exactly understand and on the basis of this contrive his death for a knowledge he possesses which is not of the highest value (secrets of the police department)" (*MOMG,* 54–55).

Indeed, Daniels's underground passage brings him face-to-face with the constant threat of death: he can easily drown in the watery sewers; he must kill a rat that bars his way (as Big Boy had to do); he stumbles upon a dead baby and dislodges it from its stuck place in the water; and he arrives in an undertaker's basement establishment at the moment a male corpse is being embalmed. At first, Daniels is a passive observer, but as he discovers his invisibility and how he can profit from it in the hidden cave, he begins to act creatively; he plots to steal money from a jewelry store safe and tools from a night watchman, and he sets about defining a space for himself. His identity also undergoes change. In the cave he gains control of his life and his past, particularly the memories of his wife, his white employer, and the policemen who had tortured him: "He possessed them now more completely than he had ever possessed them when he had lived aboveground. . . . He had no desire to go back to them" ("The Man Who Lived Underground," 536) until the humanistic dimensions of his new identity take over, for Daniels becomes an artist.

As an artist Daniels is able to give new meaning to familiar objects. He decorates his cave with one-hundred dollar bills, watches, and diamonds. The climax of this creativity comes when he performs the self-defining act of typing his name with the stolen typewriter. Michel Fabre has argued convincingly that Daniels becomes a character in his own tale. I would add that this moment of writing (even if the sentence he types began an earlier draft of the novella) also reveals Daniels's new name in the lower case, merged *"freddaniels"* (543). Farther into the story Daniels will forget his name, but the performance of writing will earn him a critical distance from the experience he is undergoing: "Just why he selected that sentence he did not know; it was merely the ritual of performing the thing that appealed to him" (548). Daniels's performance has a universalizing effect on his character. From that point on, until the story's grisly conclusion, he reverses the spatial geography of society; what was once considered civilization is now a wilderness: "that was how the world aboveground now seemed to him, a wild forest filled with death" (549). In this light "The Man Who Lived Underground" can be seen as a fugitive narrative showing man's creative response to virgin territory from which he must earn deliverance. Daniels thus sees both worlds and his own emotional ambivalence more clearly.

From his "invisible" position, Daniels enjoys some material benefits otherwise unavailable. Like Ellison's protagonist in *Invisible Man,* which owes a considerable debt to this story, Daniels tricks society by appropriating things denied him. Whereas Ellison's protagonist dwells in a cellar of a building where blacks cannot rent and steals power from the utility company, Daniels enjoys money, a visit to the cinema where he occupies "a box in the reserved section" (527), and food from Nick's Fruits and Meats. Daniels also sees innocent victims receive the same cruel treatment from police he once endured as he observes a boy and then a watchman being accused of the crimes Daniels had committed. This experience lifts Daniels's observations out of a purely racial context and into a general humanistic one, which engages his sympathies. Daniels whispers "Don't" to the watchman seconds before the latter commits suicide (558). And he comes to sing the song of the churchgoers he had earlier ridiculed: *"Glad, glad... I got Jesus in my soul"* (573). The life Daniels has seen and shared from underground teaches him love for others and gives him a message he needs to share, regardless of anyone's willingness to listen: "When I looked through all of those holes and saw how people were living, I loved 'em" (571).

Love forces Daniels to resurface and to risk rejection by society, by the church ("You can't act rowdy in God's house!" [561]), and, ultimately, by the police who reveal how threatening is his freedom: "You're free, free as air" (567). But Daniels has no wings to try that air. His awkward attempts to accelerate rushed gestures and incomprehensible phrases into flight earn him the policemen's fear that he knows their secret: "he'll squeal that we framed him" (570). When they agree to follow Daniels to his underground "home," they shoot him once he descends because he'd "wreck things" (576). Daniels succumbs at last to the watery grave he had only narrowly avoided in his initial descent. There Daniels had discovered a well of human kinship with other innocently accused people. The conflict had been motivated as much by issues of fraternity and psychology as by race.

The self-creation Daniels had engaged in, accompanying his reinvention of meaning for familiar objects, was his act of renaming and demystifying them—money, for instance, is "just like any other paper" (542)—as he renamed and reanimated himself, which was no easy task. Cross Damon, in Wright's later novel, *The Outsider* (1953), faces a similar dilemma of self-creation and self-mastery. Freed from overwhelming family and financial pressures when he survives a devastating subway accident and is presumed dead, Damon must reconstruct a life for himself. His freedom becomes his heaviest burden. "He was free from everything but himself"

(107). And, like the writer's struggle with a blank page, he must devise a narrative, create a fiction, as Daniels had done, not underground, but in real life: "What puzzled him most was that he could not think of concrete things to do. He was going to a cheap hotel in order to hide for a few days, but beyond that he had no ideas, no plans. He would have to imagine this thing out, dream it out, invent it, like a writer constructing a tale, he told himself grimly as he watched the blurred street lamps flash past the trolley's frosted window" (79). The narrative he manages to construct requires an increasingly more elaborate tapestry than he can weave, for it ever distances him from others. The device of art can fail; Damon cannot live without human contact and a story that makes connections: "He was without a name, a past, a future; no promises or pledges bound him to those about him. He had to become human before he could mingle again with people. Yet he needed those people and could become human only with them" (127). Damon, like Daniels, must risk the possibility of wrecking things by resurfacing from his "cover," or forever lose himself as a fugitive from himself. This explains, partially, why Daniels so craved human contact, why he was willing to risk rejection, even death to gain it, for these were the tests his new identity required.

Moreover, Wright felt that Daniels's real freedom came with action: his ability to improvise upon the dark, unknown, virginal territory of the cave; to handle old objects anew; and to manipulate the knowledge he gains about private and public forms of guilt, responsibility, and fraternity. This Christ-like situation did not escape Wright, who called Daniels's tragic death "brutal treatment of the superior man by his inferiors," and further, that Daniels "when he emerged from the underground was certainly talking a lot of good sense and yet in the context of the environment in which he spoke, he certainly was talking a lot of nonsense" (*MOMG,* 54-55). More than words were required. For Wright, Daniels's most important discovery was freedom of action. Here Wright's choice of setting compounds the irony because this black Everyman, the perennial fugitive from white society, must retreat to the very bowels of the city for enough distance to effect his reintegration into society. Far from the censure of blacks and the scrutiny of whites he must find a core of behavior, or performance, to demonstrate the broader, humanistic ramifications of his identity. The self that emerges from the sewers has performed a ritual of rebirth out of the muck and waste of society to heal society and himself. But he must go one step further: acting out that identity leads to more action, new performances, in the larger, more threatening theater of human society. Wright was overjoyed to have made this discovery: "The one thing that Fred Daniels did and exhibited was the *freedom of action!* As long as men have that right, the results of action will justify any attempts to save it, to protect it. Fred Daniels threw his life away, that is, when we see it from the outside; but to Fred Daniels he felt that he wanted to go and tell what he had seen, and to give testimony to what one feels is a right worth dying for. Indeed, he had the right and scope of action to feel deeply enough so that what he felt and saw acted powerfully upon him and drove him to further action" (*MOMG,* 55).

Beyond articulating a drama of self-creation and self-performance for Daniels, "The Man Who Lived Underground" turned out to be Wright's moment of personal triumph when he discovered in the act of writing a "breaking" point where the narrative "floats" and the reader begins to accept without question new developments in plot and character. "A certain *heat* is generated, like the blow of an acetelyne torch melting metals and fusing them together in one" (*MOMG,* 44). Such writing drew Wright into the kind of improvisation he saw so favorably in Daniels's behavior, pulling together the disparate objects he finds into a new meaningful relationship to him and his cave underground. Wright quickly grasped this moment of narrative invention to integrate conflicting elements of his own tormented past, particularly, the legacy from his grandmother, and the knowledge he had acquired by his reading, listening to music, and engaging himself in the world since her death in 1934. Wright wanted to reach that heat-generating breaking point—which he does in *Black Boy*—so that the act of writing would become the improvisational performance of the author's freedom of action, his leap into the air: "From the character's point of view this breaking, in my opinion, represents a point in life where the past falls away and the character must, in order to go on living, fling himself upon the face of the formless night and create a world, a *new* world, in which we live. To me—rightly or wrongly—the hallmark of good writing resides precisely in this sense of creating the *new,* the *freedom* and the *need* and the *desire* to create this new" (*MOMG,* 45). Wright went so far as to compare "The Man Who Lived Underground" to jazz music in which improvisation creates a new whole. The inventive exhilaration he felt in writing this fiction, particularly in his coming to terms with a past that now had meaning in his ability to control and present it through language, contributes to making the novella one of the most important works in Wright's canon.

Ellison's Visible Geography. "We can hope to be eagles, can't we? Can't we?"

The publication of Wright's novella along with Ralph Ellison's story "Flying Home" in the anthology *Cross Section* (1944) offers a rarely acknowledged link between the two texts that critics have overlooked, focusing instead on affinities and contrasts between *Black Boy* and *Invisible Man*. Robert Stepto has argued that Ellison's novel effectively challenged Wright's hold on interpretations of black rural and urban culture (or the lack thereof, in Wright's distorted view), and Joseph T. Skerrett, Jr., has examined Ellison's unconscious psychological, if not aesthetic, debt to Wright. Anthology editor Edwin Seaver was more prophetic than he realized in introducing Ellison among "new" writers in the back pages following Wright's contribution. Seen together these stories establish Ellison's early challenge to Wright through his antithetical metaphors of spatial mobility and different acts of performance that affirm rather than deny a base for black cultural expression.

The underside of society where Daniels freely affirms human kinship is reversed yet similarly resolved in "Flying Home." Todd, a young black aviator on a training flight who, incidentally, fulfills Bigger Thomas's dream in *Native Son* ("I could fly a plane if I had a chance"), crash lands in a southern field and must recover on ground level the racial identity and cultural community he had hoped to escape in his too speedy ascent. Thrusting too quickly, climbing too high, Todd's plane collided with a flock of buzzards called "jimcrows" (157), which brought him down to earth in more ways than one. Injured with a broken ankle, Todd is found by the old man Jefferson, who tells him a folktale until help arrives. Todd learns from Jefferson's tale forms of cultural behavior to help him avoid the doom represented by the arrival of Mr. Graves, the white owner of the land and the figure of death and burial. Graves sums up his threat by saying, "You all know you cain't let the nigguh git up that high without his going crazy. The nigguh brain ain't built right for high altitudes" (168). Todd performs his own act to deflect racial hostility away from his career as a fighter pilot, which would, we assume, "wreck things." Todd is carted off in a straight jacket with the same dismissal Lawson and Murphy showed when they tried to "reason" with Daniels. Crucial to both stories is the image of the protagonist's complex and often ambiguous relation to the black cultural landscape. The spatial imagery constructed by Wright and Ellison provides layers of contrasts within the ascent-descent angle of public and private achievement.

Daniels begins at ground level and descends into the sewer, both the bowels and the womb of the city. He resurfaces only to get shot in the very tunnel that gave him rebirth. Todd begins at an altitude achieved by flight training until Jim Crow, the reality of black life in the South, catches up with him and reminds him of the racism that keeps black pilots out of heroic combat. "Stretched painfully upon the ground" (151), Todd encounters the charged field of racial etiquette that keeps blacks grounded in dependency and sharecropping. Jefferson himself admits, "I got no where to go . . . an' they'd come after me if I did" (166). Todd's fall prepares him to experience the "time and space" of a black reality he had avoided until now through overcompensation. His girlfriend had once warned him: "Don't you be contented to prove over and over again that you're brave or skillful just because you're black" (153). Todd must learn to replace the artificial dignity he assumes from his flight-training—"It's the only dignity I have. . . . It's the most meaningful act in the world" (154, 155)—with the more artful survival Jefferson teaches him to practice on the heavily mined field of race relations.

Jefferson's folktale about his trip to heaven and his misuse of angel wings in flashy acrobatic flight, which gets him expelled from heaven, is a classic cautionary tale, the moral lesson of which does not escape the errant Todd. But the tale on another level is the source of Jefferson's ability to deal with racial hostility in the South: it is his flight of imagination, his creativity, his inner personality undiminished by the hostile social customs threatening him and Todd. Jefferson's performance of the tale to the naive Todd, prefiguring Trueblood's tale-telling in *Invisible Man,* leads Todd to understand the extent of his evasion of identity and kinship with the land. Back on the ground Todd can mount his own performance to stave off death—Mr. Graves—through his display of feigned insanity: "Blasts of hot, hysterical laughter tore from his chest, causing his eyes to pop and he felt that the veins in his neck would surely burst. And then a part of him stood behind it all, watching the surprise in Graves's red face and his own hysteria" (169). What Todd creates here is the device or mask of the "Little Man" he had observed to exist behind Jefferson's obsequious "peasant" behavior with Mr. Graves.

This performance gives Todd an ironic distance from his present unfortunate circumstance of failing the training mission and meeting the hostility of whites who want to keep blacks in their place. The lesson Jefferson imparts urges Todd to apply vernacular knowledge as well as scientific knowledge to have a successful flight. Once completing this performance, thereby establishing his cultural membership, Todd is able to *hear* the song hummed by Jefferson's grandson and to realize that a buzzard can bring a knowledge worth its weight in gold: "Then like a song within his head he heard the boy's soft humming and saw the dark bird glide into the sun and glow like a bird of flaming gold" (170).

Ellison and Wright lead their protagonists to new heights of mobility: a descent in "The Man Who Lived Underground" becomes an altitude of ascent, and a too quick ascent in "Flying Home" requires a descent to ground level or wilderness testing to achieve greater heights. Both authors invert the values associated with certain geographical figuration to establish metaphors for their protagonists' struggle to uncover a sometimes hidden cultural landscape and, upon reaching it, to perform self-creating acts.

A more elaborate gesture of self-creation takes place in *Invisible Man* where the narrator recreates his entire life in the form of the novel he relates from his cellar retreat. The novel, more than Daniels's short story or Todd's moment of delirium and heard song, becomes the principal literary creation, or performance, born of a protagonist and a writer's collaborative refuge. *Invisible Man* is filled with performances of every kind: the Battle Royal, Homer Barbee's oration, Lucius Brockway's ritualistic stoking of the furnace, Todd Clifton's displays of Sambo dolls for sale, and sexual dalliances that confuse the "ass struggle with the class struggle." The most instructive performance is Trueblood's telling the tale of his incest, because in so doing he repeats on a grand scale the initiatory performance that instructs as well as captivates the nameless protagonist.

Trueblood's spoken language begins realistically, becomes psychological, and ends with Trueblood's transcendence of his guilt and shame by his internalizing the blues. He teaches the protagonist the essence of storytelling on the lower frequencies (which can also refer to the "low" subject of the tale). Such storytelling has the ability to change the social and moral status of the teller (just as slaves songs did, as shown in Chapter 1) by transforming him into an exemplary figure who confronts his fate, accepts it, and transcends it through the art of his high talk. Trueblood has a lesson to impart to others; although his principal audience is Mr. Norton, the main beneficiary is the naive protagonist. Trueblood's story becomes as subversive as the novel because it speaks *for* Norton and *to* the protagonist. Trueblood's survival through storytelling (his moral redemption by facing up to his guilt as well as the remuneration he gets simply by telling the tale) is a lesson for the narrator in the same way that Jefferson's tale imparts a survival tactic for Todd in "Flying Home," who had to be pulled *down* to those lower frequencies he had tried to forget. Those lower frequencies are what earn him a level of control high enough to escape the grave. The invisible man's final line in the novel—"Who knows but that, on the lower frequencies, I speak for you" (439)—suggests also that he has found a place in narrative on which to base his claims to a humanistic, universal landscape: the broad terrain of verbal art that is the novel. His performance of the narrative, like Trueblood's telling of the tale, earns him an audience and kinship with the reader. An early microcosm of this movement can be seen when the protagonist makes his first, extemporaneous speech protesting the eviction of the Harlem couple, who harbor among their possessions the key to the protagonist's kinship with them: their freedom papers, signaling their transformative history. The protagonist's speech changes him into a leader and spokesperson. Although he is later manipulated by the Brotherhood into speaking *for* them, his recounting of the event in his performance of the narrative (or novel) teaches the protagonist-storyteller-writer how he can change himself through language as Trueblood has done. In a flash of narrative play and insight, he pulls the reader into kinship with him; writer and reader, teller and listener, become one. Trueblood is Norton on those ever-widening lower frequencies. If it is Ellison's goal to affirm an interracial kinship that the American psyche finds threatening, wherein black and white Americans share more than racism allows either to admit or to enjoy, then we know why the invisible man never resurfaces. He must remain underground, tease us with the promise (the threat?) of his return aboveground. Otherwise, we may kill him for his humanism: he'd wreck things.

In addition to examining cultural and geographical transition in the protagonist's movement from the North to the South and back North again, *Invisible Man* offers a structural movement from prologue to narrative to epilogue as a way of passing in and out of time and space. The novel also presents the geometrical figure of the boomerang as a metaphor for the passage and progress of the hero. The boomerang may be Ellison's version of the suspended arcs that introduce Kabnis's story in *Cane.* Structurally, Ellison's novel is a boomerang. As a device used against the protagonist's naivete about what keeps this "nigger boy running," it turns back upon the reader and to the novel's starting point when we realize both prologue and epilogue are set in the underground. A boomerang does more than simply return to its starting point; it is either a weapon or a tool according to its often unseen cutting edge. Once Ellison launches the novel as a familiar *bildungsroman* of one individual, he shows readers the surrealistic cutting edge of black experience not aboveground, where it is subject to societal guises such as those adopted by Rinehart, but on "the lower frequencies" (the underground itself or the moaning bass notes of a blues melody) where the narrator's voice can grow large enough to speak "for you." The reader, that elusive but inclusive *you,* is captured as the arc of the verbal boomerang lifts from the aesthetically fertile underground. Geometry meets geography.

If Ellison's protagonist follows Daniels so closely, creating not only his own character but also the novel of *Invisible Man,* then why is his fate so different? The voice Fred Daniels had attained went unheard by both the white policemen who shot him and the black churchgoers who were offended by his trail of sewer mud and filth. Blacks and whites were deaf to Daniels's truth. Ellison's hero survives for two reasons: first, readers need him to relate the novel, which is narrated retrospectively; second, Ellison diverts the listener away from his protagonist's truth-telling. By skillfully reserving until the very last line of the novel how the speaker merges himself with his audience ("I speak for you"), Ellison lets readers realize the protagonist's truth-telling too late to stop him. It overtakes us. Ellison subverts our tendency to silence or kill the truth, and the protagonist has the last word. The novel's closure is the protagonist's survival. Only by beating his listeners to the punch, as it were, does he secure voice and authority.

Hibernation cannot remain a viable form of survival, however, for the heart and mind, as Wright has shown, demand fulfillment through human contact. Furthermore, hibernation promotes inertia and inaction, despite all the invisible man's words to the contrary. As an antidote to Ellison's ever-spiraling boomerang, Toni Morrison (discussed in Chapter 6) offers the trajectory of flight. Before Morrison's fiction articulates its angle of ascent, LeRoi Jones further dramatizes the limits of underground hibernation and stasis in his play *Dutchman* (1964).

Jones's protagonist Clay fails to reclaim the cultural authority Lula has usurped from him. His tragic encounter with Lula in an roaring subway car underground was forseen in an obscure, but revealing passage in *Invisible Man.* When Ellison's protagonist leaves the factory hospital after being told he isn't "prepared for work under our industrial conditions" (187), he travels to Harlem by subway: "Across the aisle a young platinum blonde nibbled at a red Delicious apple as station lights rippled past behind her. The train plunged. I dropped through the roar, giddy and vacuum-minded, sucked under and put into late afternoon Harlem" (190). Were it not for Mary Rambo's southern hospitality in Harlem, the invisible man would have succumbed to the tragic fate awaiting Clay, who is similarly naive and malleable. If we regard Mary Rambo's character as partly developed from the section edited out of *Invisible Man* and published later as the short story, "Out of the Hospital and Under the Bar," then we see Rambo as a supportive listener who requires artful storytelling before she will help the protagonist escape his confinement. She encourages verbal dexterity in his rendering of the tale of heroism that landed him in the hospital. He must give the tale just the right embellishment to gain her sympathy; she requires him to perform the same kind of cultural mapmaking that Trueblood and Jefferson required their attentive but reluctant protégés to do to carry on the tradition. In *Dutchman* Clay allows Lula to draw the map for him, giving her far too much control over the underground.

LeRoi Jones. The Device of Descent/Dissent: "The Bottom where the Colored lived . . . squatted in this actual wilderness"

Heir to both Ellison and Wright, LeRoi Jones (a.k.a. Amiri Baraka) starts from a different point than Wright's now familiar alienation "between the world and me," or the invisible man's promised rise from underground. Jones places himself directly in the world, vulnerable to all its temptations of various, conflicting ideologies (from Bohemianism to Black Nationalism to Marxism), sexual preferences (from bisexuality to heterosexuality), and aesthetic influences (from the Beat poets to jazz composers). Jones moves among them by donning several masks and devices to ensure his mobility beyond the inertia, or hibernation, imposed by race or class:

> I am a soul in the world: in
> the world of my soul the whirled
> light / from the day
> the sacked land
> of my father.
>
> .   .   .   .
> The day of my soul, is
> the nature of that
> place. It is a landscape. Seen
> from the top of a hill. A

grey expanse; dull fires
throbbing on its seas.

(*"The invention of comics,"*
The Dead Lecturer, 37)

In two key works Jones probes the landscape of that soul; the "grey expanse" and throbbing dull fires turn out to be areas of sexual conflict. His play *Dutchman* and his only novel to date, *The System of Dante's Hell* (1965), use descent into the underground as a means of unmasking the various devices that tempt protagonists to ignore or deny their sexual and cultural identities. The reality beneath the subway's "modern myth" in the play leads to the tragic unveiling of Clay's device of assimilation. In the novel, Roi's descent into the Bottom black community near the Air Force base in Louisiana brings him to a partial awakening of consciousness. Both results come from key performances by the protagonists that determine their separate fates.

Although scholars have puzzled over the enigmatic title of Jones's best known play and, some may argue, his most fully achieved work, most have neglected its reference to the realm of art in favor of history. Most critics have cited *Dutchman* as a reference either to the Dutch trading vessel that brought the first Africans to the New World in 1619, or to Jones's innovative use of Wagner's opera *The Flying Dutchman* as a way of seeing both Lula and Clay trapped in a curse of historical inevitability. The realm of crafts offers a simple, yet compelling and useful definition, especially if the underground is seen as a stage for performances of identity. In carpentry, a dutchman is an "odd piece inserted to fill an opening, hide a defect, or strengthen a weak part," or it can be a "*device* for hiding or counteracting structural defects." In set design, it is "the strip of cloth used to conceal the crack between two scenery flats." As the accursed captain of a doomed ship in search of safe harbor, Lula, who commands the docile passengers, certainly goads Clay into filling her opening, but Clay himself is full of other devices and guises meant to mask his feelings of inferiority or the apparent structural "flaw" of his blackness: his three-button sports jacket, his pretentions to the poetic status of Baudelaire. These contrivances (like Ellison's subversive narrative closure) keep Clay alive, but not for long.

Both Clay and Lula appear to have entered the subway expecting passage. Clay is on his way to a party; Lula is looking for a good time and a victim. Underground, away from society, each is a well-known type. Lula eats apples and Clay shifts about uncomfortably in his three-button jacket ("What've you got that jacket and tie on in all this heat for?" [18]), which allow both of them to be seen and unseen at the same time. Lula clearly spots Clay as a "tender big-eyed prey" (29), and he has eyed her, Lula claims, "in the vicinity of my ass and legs" (7). These gestures and clothes mask an invisible, hidden truth that begins to unravel when Clay and Lula enter into a verbal sexual joust, molded largely from Clay's apparent passivity. Their mutual invisibility seems to Lula a good reason to escape history: "And we'll pretend the people cannot see you. That is, the citizens. And that you are free of your own history. And I am free of my history. We'll pretend that we are both anonymous beauties smashing along through the city's entrails" (21). The pretense masks the impossibility of avoiding history, the past of slavery or the present state of sexual and political domination, which prevents Clay and Lula from meeting as "beauties." Both are on dangerous ground in a ship of state going nowhere. Jones's imagery here suggests that both characters are struggling to escape a wilderness of sorts, yet only dimly perceive its ever-constricting enclosure. Lula is a self-described predator, Lena the Hyena; Clay her big-eyed prey.

Imagining themselves to be out of the underground they never really escape, Lula wants to lead Clay *up* "the narrow steps of a tenement" (20) where *high* "above the street and ignorant cowboys" they will make love in her "dark living room" (25). Lula continues: "And you'll call my rooms black as a grave. You'll say, 'This place is like Juliet's tomb' " (26). Thus Lula presumes to define Clay's actions, to talk about his manhood, direct it, chart it: "I'll make you a map of it. Just as soon as we get to my house" (26). The underground, however, takes them on a different course. In this sexual wilderness, Lula and Clay resort to behavior meant to relieve each of pretense and device and history. Clay, as Lula accuses him, could be, like the slave narrators, "an escaped nigger" who "crawled through the wire and made tracks to my side" (29). Clay's repartee points out areas of confinement other than plantations: "You must be Jewish. All you can think about is wire" (29). Yet again they fail to realize they are trapped in the limited space of the subway (a metaphor for the history they cannot escape) groaning on its subterranean journey, the destination of which remains unknown and unquestioned. Nor is Lula able to see who Clay really is outside the routine of her nightly prowls and hunger for apples. Clay is a kind of invisible man who frustrates Lula's expectations for sexual coupling and conquest. Lula muses, "Except I do go on as I do. Apples and long walks with deathless intelligent lovers. But you mix it up. Look out the window, all the time. Turning pages. Change change change. Till, shit, I don't know you. Wouldn't, for that matter. You're too serious" (28). Lula tries to arouse Clay to her kind of action or participatory performance when she dances wildly through the subway aisles and abuses Clay by calling him an Uncle Tom, "Uncle Thomas Woolly Head" (32). When Clay slaps her, he unmasks the surfaces between them. He reveals the contours of his hidden culture, which remain invisible to Lula: "Belly rub is not Queens. Belly rub is dark places, with big hats and overcoats held up with one arm. Belly rub hates you" (34). This alternative place of cultural refuge is not on the map Lula thought she could draw of Clay's background or of his manhood.

Clay, for his part, may have wanted a place for sexual performance in upper rooms, "high above the streets," but the real test is down in the subway. He must get rid of the guise of the three-button jacket (as we will see Milkman Dead do in Chapter 6), which is his most visible device—his dutchman. And he must use words that unmask the devices of language. Clay's elaborate discourse on the blues reveals it to be just such a hidden mechanism, as much a weapon as a device (like Ellison's boomerang) that conceals rage while it projects rage. Clay also repeats the boomerang effect on the mythic grounds below (the underground here being the hidden terrain of black culture) by turning with much verbal fury against Lula, who had intended to manipulate his sexual interest in her. The ejaculation of desire Lula expected turns out to be an outburst of an identity that thwarts Lula's devices of seduction and castration. Clay's extended verbal solo is his performance of hidden identity, whose sudden visibility is menacing: "You don't know anything except what's there for you to see. An Act. Lies. Device. Not the pure heart, the pumping black heart" (34), which is the "defect" requiring a dutchman to protect and to hide it. Clay goes on in spite of himself, tragically erring by exposing his black heart in all its exuberance: "You don't ever know that. And I sit here, in this buttoned-up suit, to keep myself from cutting all your throats. I mean wantonly" (34). Music, in the same manner, was a device for Bessie Smith and Charlie Parker: "If Bessie Smith had killed some white people she wouldn't have needed that music. She could have talked very straight and plain about the world. No metaphors. No grunts. No wiggles in the dark of her soul. Just straight two and two are four. . . . Charlie Parker . . . would've played not a note of music if he just walked up to East Sixty-seventh Street and killed the first ten white people he saw . . . all it needs is a simple knife thrust. Just let me bleed you, you loud whore, and one poem vanished" (35). Literature itself is just as ironic a device as music.

Lula, however, cannot accept this pumping black heart. She, like others in Clay's audience, prefers metaphor, device, dutchman, which allows her and the dominant culture to manipulate others. The naked truth behind the device would "wreck things." This is why Lula kills Clay and why she remains trapped in the routine of eating apples and courting sacrificial lovers. She and Clay are victims: Clay because he dies, Lula because she cannot die until she finally accepts and loves the messy soil of humanity beneath the surface. Another poem by Jones in his collection *The Dead Lecturer* speaks to this agony:

> This is the enclosure (flesh,
> where innocence is a weapon. An
> abstraction. Touch. (Not mine.
> Or yours, if you are the soul I had
> and abandoned when I was blind and had
> my enemies carry me as a dead man
>
> . . . .
>
> *("An Agony. As Now,"* 15)

A different kind of subterranean sexual conflict appears in *The System of Dante's Hell,* a novel overlooked because of its experimental form or perhaps because the protagonist Roi, a homosexual, probes the depths of same-sex lust as an ironic metaphor for his evasion of self-love. By situating Roi among the heretics in the "deepest part of hell" (7), the author sets the stage for an elaborate performance of self through sexuality on the "lower frequencies" of place and personality, the black community of the Bottom. Whereas Lula is a female Mr. Graves, who wants to keep blacks in their place and map out their behavior, and whereas Clay may have missed the dark room above, but found his sweltering grave below, the characters in *The System of Dante's Hell* reverse these spatial images and actions. Roi's principal antagonist in "The Heretics" section of the novel is the black woman Peaches, who goads Roi briefly away from homosexuality and forces him to perform sexually what Clay had accomplished verbally. Instead of making love high above the city, Roi has sex in the Bottom, which is, paradoxically, the only height this Air Force flyer achieves. Although trained for combat as a gunner, Roi, like Ellison's Todd, is grounded by his evasion of cultural identity and, in this case, heterosexuality.

The novel follows two lines of development. One is the narrative of Roi's upbringing from childhood through adolescence to adulthood. At the novel's close, he is an Air Force gunner on a night's jaunt to the Bottom, seeking sexual pleasure wherever he can find it. The second line of development is a spatial tension contrasting the protagonist's chronological growing *up* with his gradual moral *decline* through levels of sin until he reaches the deepest part of hell at the *height* of his maturation. The choices Roi has made through the years have led him to commit the basest evil. "It is heresy, against one's own sources, running in terror, from one's deepest responses and insights . . . the denial of feelings," the author explains, "that I see as basest evil" (7). Like the aviator Todd, Roi's sin of heresy requires him to enter the lower depths of ancestral territory to achieve self-awareness. This point of argument projects ahead to Toni Morrison's protagonist Jadine in *Tar Baby,* who runs away from and fails to recognize "her true and ancient properties" (305) in the dual sense to mean the racial traits and the physical territory or property that establish grounds of mutual possession. Jones's Roi is searching for a place for his person throughout the novel, "Your own space, wherever" (37). He will discover, much to his bewilderment, "I am myself after all" (59), echoing the invisible man's realization, "I am nobody but myself." Before this occurs, however, readers are plunged into Roi's confused past. *The System of Dante's Hell* is the system of Roi's initiation into sexual and cultural performance beyond the demands of his technical or military training. The restrictions he had placed on himself make him an Air Force gunner who is nearly impotent.

Like Todd in Ellison's "Flying Home," Roi had imagined his aviator career as a means of escaping the "low" aspects of black reality. His skill as a flyer is also illusory, for it is predicated upon assimilation and escape: "My soul is white, pure white, and soars" (70), which echoes the artificial "dignity" Todd found in his flight training and reveals Ellison's brilliant inversion of space (as region and as atmosphere) and skills. Todd needs the vernacular technology transmitted through Jefferson's folktale to get himself off the ground, which is what Roi will learn from Peaches. Roi doesn't realize the extent to which his homosexuality grounds him, encloses him in passivity and inertia: "My cold sin in the cities . . . my fear of my own death's insanity, and an actual longing for men that brooded in each finger of my memory" (125). He admits, "I've been fucked in the ass. I love books and smells and my own voice" (131). Roi's homosexuality, rather than being a celebration of masculine autonomy as in Baldwin's *Go Tell It on the Mountain,* is a longing for personal contact beyond the narcissism he dislikes but is powerless to change: "To be pushed under a quilt, and call it love. To shit water for days and say I've been loved. Been warm. A real thing in the world. Seen my shadow. My reflection. I'm here, alive. Touch me. Please. Please, touch me" (138-39).

In search of the touch, Roi encounters the gender he has rejected, which is the probable source of his redemption. He is touched by Peaches in the Bottom of Shreveport, Louisiana (*down* South). But it is an aggressive, vengeful touch before it becomes a healing embrace, for Roi, in his youth, had passed through upper levels of hell or sin before arriving here. The previous events are cut from the same wrinkled cloth, such as the homosexual coupling between characters known only as 46 and 64, figures of inversion and self-dialogue, who establish Roi's narcissism and inner conflict ("Am I like that?"). At another time the author is critical of Roi and his teenage friends in the chapter "Treachery to Kindred" when they pick up a black woman, abuse her, and threaten her with rape. Black women are described individually as either "some sentry of Africa" or "Some short-haired witch out of my mother's most hideous dreams" (130). The exploitative acts Roi commits as an adolescent further doom him to the sin of heresy and restrict his later ambitions for heroic flight as an aviator. He expects least of all that Peaches, one of the black women of the Bottom and on the bottom, will avenge his abuse of women and his negative view of the ancestral South ("a world for aztecs lost on the bone side of the mountain," and "a culture of violence and foodsmells" [121]) when she all but *rapes* Roi: "Goddamn punk, You gonna fuck me tonight or I'm gonna pull your fuckin dick aloose" (140).

Roi's problematic and unwilling coupling with Peaches recalls Kabnis's frustrated *walpurgisnacht* and play-acting in Fred Halsey's cellar when he fails to consummate his sexual interest in Cora and ends up being mothered. Peaches prevails when she grabs Roi by the balls and commands him to perform sexually and to jettison his "ideas" or the device of words (such as Clay used). Peaches finds Roi adequate, but not satisfying, good "even on a sof. But I still got to teach you" (146). The performance required of Roi in the Bottom is more than sexual, it is cultural. He is drawn, momentarily, out of his homosexual indulgences (as when he later refuses a male offer of fellatio), he is forced to stop talking white or "norf," and he is goaded into sharing watermelon for breakfast and a meal of greens and knuckles. As he becomes known briefly as "Peaches' man" in the greetings of neighbors, who acknowledge him with a "Hey" (149), he struts proudly *up* the road.

Roi begins to change: "I cursed Chicago. . . . All lies before, I thought. All fraud and sickness" (148). His plunge to the very bottom of the Bottom leads him to a height greater than any he had experienced as an Air Force recruit. Roi leaves Peaches with a gesture of self-redemption following his difficult and mildly successful intercourse with her: "leaping in the air like I saw heroes do in flicks" (143). This brief moment of self-achievement is rendered less dramatically than Milkman Dead's leap in *Song of Solomon*, but the key elements pitting blind acceptance of technological training and assimilation against cultural identification and personal triumph are present nonetheless. Peaches's aggressive lovemaking is what elevates Roi to consciousness.

Underground spaces of sewers, cellars, and subways have thus become stages primarily for male protagonists to resolve dilemmas associated with their ability or inability to assume responsibilities to race, culture, and family. Perhaps it is basically a conceit of male writers that the earth, like a woman, must be possessed. Wright, Ellison, and LeRoi Jones have created protagonists who penetrate underground regions with the urgency of sexual conquest; yet they end up being possessed by those very environments. The underground has its own score to settle. Peaches, the "pilot" of Roi's deliverance, shows us that women characters as well as women writers may view the environment differently, may carve out "womanist" landscapes to create new myths about place, person, and performance. For these we need to look to Zora Neale Hurston, Alice Walker, and Gayl Jones, who reveal the kind of geography that redeems both men and women.

CHAPTER FOUR

Keep me from sinking down: Zora Neale Hurston, Alice Walker, and Gayl Jones

Whatever rocky soil [my mother] landed on, she turned
into a garden.

—Alice Walker

Images of place and performance, landscape and identity in texts
by several black women writers may well overturn the aesthetic primacy of
the subterranean worlds depicted by Wright, Ellison, and LeRoi Jones. Alice
Walker, for one, offers a *womanist* view of female "place" in society. As
defined in Walker's collection of essays, *In Search of Our Mothers' Gardens:
Womanist Prose* (1983), womanist describes "outrageous, audacious,
courageous, or willful behavior . . . committed to survival and wholeness of
entire people, male and female" (xi). Walker further defines the term
through an intriguing proportional analogy: "womanist is to feminist as
purple is to lavender." As derived from the expression "womanish," a direct
tie can be seen to a moment in one of Zora Neale Hurston's early stories,
"Drenched in Light," when the protagonist, Isis, is chastised for inviting
adventure from the gatepost near her house. "Youse too 'oomanish jumpin'
up in everybody's face dat pass" (*Spunk,* 9). Whether or not we accept this
definition of postfeminism, it proves useful in considering the poles of
geographical settings and imagery some women writers have used to chart
their protagonists' struggle for voice and self-possession.

Zora Neale Hurston takes readers to the horizon and back in the story of
Janie Starks's audacious trek to the muck of the Florida Everglades, which
secures for her a new place in the community to which she returns. Alice
Walker shapes one character, Meridian, into a compass, charting the ances-

tral terrain of blacks and Indians where grace comes from acknowledging the spiritual significance of burial grounds. In a later novel, Walker examines female oppression and geographical distance in the lives of two estranged sisters, one in the American South, the other in West Africa. Gayl Jones examines the claustrophobic interiors of a rented room or a prison cell as her characters' grope for meaning in the performance of a blues song or in the act of murder (one gesture is simply the fulfillment of the other, an argument similar to the one advanced in LeRoi Jones's *Dutchman:* "if Bessie Smith had killed some white folks, she wouldn't have needed that music"). These writers encourage performances of new identities in new spaces: front porches for Hurston, petunia gardens or cemeteries for Walker, pubs or prison cells for Gayl Jones. The settings become finely honed womanist landscapes as they audaciously and outrageously pull readers up from the underground and toward a new geographical idiom, startling in its simplicity: a mother's garden, which, Walker assures us, nurtures art: "I remember people coming to my mother's yard to be given cuttings from her flowers; I hear again the praise showered on her because whatever rocky soil she landed on, she turned into a garden. A garden so brilliant with colors, so original in its design, so magnificent with life and creativity that to this day people drive by our house in Georgia—perfect strangers and imperfect strangers—and ask to stand or walk among my mother's art" (241). As if to solidify an already strong tie between herself and Zora Neale Hurston, Walker once inquired about Hurston's love for flowers. An elderly informant, Hurston's neighbor, replied: "She was crazy about them. And she was a great gardener" (114).

Zora Neale Hurston. "Throw up a highway through de wilderness"

Hurston began writing during the period of the Harlem Renaissance and published short fiction in *Crisis* and *Opportunity.* Like Claude McKay, Hurston loved black folk life and found the high ingredients of civilization and culture among the "lowlife." Like Ray's experiences in the Ditch of Marseilles, Janie Mae Crawford, the protagonist of Hurston's best-known novel, *Their Eyes Were Watching God* (1937), discovers her full voice and autonomy in the lowlands, down in the Florida muck, from which she rises rather than sinks. Long concerned with spatial relations as well as the prevailing erroneous assumptions about social class, Hurston gives compelling expression to relations between geography and identity.

Hurston's central subject has been her consistent depiction of life in Eatonville, Florida, the all-black town where she grew up and where most of her fiction including *Their Eyes Were Watching God* takes place. Her autobiography, the title of which defines her preference for mobility, *Dust Tracks on a Road* (1942), begins with the founding of Eatonville and its incorporation as a town. Not until the book's third chapter does the author introduce herself. Clearly in Hurston's view this geography and the socio-political significance of an all-black town where her father as mayor authored some of the legislation shaped her identity and her art. Hurston's South presents neither a Toomeresque swan song, nor a Wrightian sense of doom. Daughter of the landowning Potts family on her mother's side and of the landless Hurstons on her father's side, she was acutely aware of the importance of land and ancestry. Hurston endows her fiction with a consciousness of space and place and their impact on personal growth. Her strong sense of rootedness has generated some controversy. Most writers of her time wanted to reject the South because of its racism; few wanted to celebrate its flourishing black culture. This fact as well as Hurston's unabashed "womanist" behavior must have endeared her to Alice Walker, born in Eatonton, Georgia, who discovered a fellow writer and "homegirl." This notion of passing on an artistic and geographical legacy has its roots in Hurston's best novel.

Their Eyes Were Watching God concerns Janie Mae Crawford's growth to maturity out of her relationships with four men: Johnny Taylor, who kissed the adolescent Janie and made her aging grandmother, Nanny, wary of her blossoming sexuality and fearful for her probable exploitation by men ("De nigger woman is de mule uh de world so fur as Ah can see" [29]); Logan Killicks, who marries Janie with Nanny's blessings for the security of his property; Jody Starks, who takes Janie away from Killicks and to a new all-black town where he establishes himself as mayor; and "Tea Cake" Vergible Woods, who wins Janie's heart following Jody's death, and who takes her with him among the migrant workers in the lowlands of the Everglades. While trying to save Janie during a violent flood, Tea Cake is bitten by a rabid dog. When he too becomes rabid and attacks Janie, she kills him in self-defense. Janie returns to Eatonville, faces a barrage of gossip and envy, and tells her story to her best friend and neighbor, Pheoby Watson.

Janie's storytelling establishes the novel's inner performance and outer narrative frame. Janie provides Pheoby with more than just the details of her adventure with Tea Cake; she reveals the history of her family and the cultural sanction for her newly found freedom: "T'aint no use in me telling you somethin' unless Ah give you de understanding to go 'long wid it" (19). Her storytelling also introduces the principal spatial metaphors shaping Janie's development as stages in the attainment of voice and self-possession. In this manner Hurston depicts various kinds of wilderness.

Nanny's advice to Janie early in the novel sets the trajectory of personality and performance in motion. Nanny reminisces about her longtime dream of preaching a great sermon about "colored women sitting on high, but they wasn't no pulpit for [her]" (32). As Nanny recounts her experience of motherhood during slavery, which changed the course of her life, the innocent tale becomes a legacy, indeed a cultural document or text: "Freedom found me wid a baby daughter in mah arms, so Ah said Ah'd take a broom and a cookpot and throw up a highway through de wilderness for her" (32). The wilderness is both literal and figurative. When the mistress suspects the truth that Nanny's child is also the master's, she threatens to sell the baby. Nanny and the child escape the plantation and confront the wilds: "In de black dark Ah wrapped mah baby de best Ah knowed how and made it to de swamp by de river. Ah knowed de place was full uh moccasins and other bitin' snakes, but Ah was more skeered uh whut was behind me. Ah hide in dere day and night and suckled de baby every time she start to cry, for fear somebody might hear her and Ah'd git found. . . . De noise uh de owls skeered me; de limbs of dem cypress trees took to crawlin' and movin' round after dark, and two three times Ah heered panthers prowlin' round. But nothin' never hurt me 'cause de Lawd knowed how it was" (35).

Nanny's tale of deliverance links to the escape episode in many fugitive slave narratives. By integrating the early Afro-American literary form into the novel, Hurston provides a cultural context for Janie's contemporary quest. Furthermore, Nanny's confrontation with nature at its harshest and most fearful level anticipates and foreshadows Janie's turmoil during a flood. This parallel will be examined later. When Nanny's daughter, Leafy, suffers rape, becomes pregnant, and succumbs to alcohol and drifting, she "gets lost off the highway" of Nanny's dream. Janie is next in line to hear this sermon, to receive Nanny's text: "Whilst Ah was tendin' you of nights Ah said Ah'd save the text for you." Janie is thus admonished to better herself: "Ah been waitin' a long time, Janie, but nothin' Ah been through ain't too much if you just take a stand on high ground lak Ah dreamed" (32). Although Janie will take several detours from Nanny's highway in the course of the novel, she will not get lost; she learns at the novel's close just how urgently her life and Tea Cake's depend on reaching high ground. Nanny's advice is heeded, ironically, after all. And the text Nanny had saved for Janie becomes the kernel of the narrative Janie will recount to Pheoby, making Pheoby a suitable heir to the same legacy. This idea of matrilinear heritage also appears as a motif in later works by Gayl Jones and Toni Morrison. Today's readers may view Hurston's novel as a reminder to conserve an emotional and cultural landscape.

Hurston skillfully posits two different views of geography, place, and personality. She contrasts Nanny's desire for land as a means of security with Janie's broader search for land*scape,* indeed Janie's escape from land (Killicks's sixty acres) into the wider possibilities of geography that offer leadership (Jody's office of mayor) and autonomy (Tea Cake's free spirit). Hurston replaces Nanny's idea of social class conferring high or low status with Janie's preferable and dynamic arc of travel between the two. Here Hurston comes close to uniting the seemingly irreconcilable arcs of racial and geographical consciousness found in *Cane.* Nanny's admission that "us colored folks is branches without roots," which makes things in her view "come round in queer ways" (31), becomes a geometrical figure echoing the threat of incompleteness or indeterminacy that stalls in *Cane* and prefiguring Ellison's metaphor of the boomerang. Hurston suggests that roads traveled fully lead not only from low to high ground, but also can take us, as Janie's road does, from the sweltering depths of a culture's swampland to a reconquered, redefined place in the home.

The movement from the muck back to the porch inaugurates Janie's most important performance whereby she reenters the community as a new woman. Her friend Pheoby, the eager transmitting agent of this new identity, becomes Janie's disciple. Pheoby's "hungry listening" (23) encourages Janie to tell the story well. Having passed through the "intimate gate" to Janie's more private back porch, Pheoby becomes Janie's mouthpiece to the less enlightened community gossips, who hold court on their more public front porches: "You can tell 'em what Ah say if you wants to. Dat's just de same as me 'cause mah tongue is in mah friend's mouf" (17). Janie's storytelling ability and Pheoby's attention help both women reach an elevated place of triumph over gender-restricted social place: "Ah done growed ten feet higher from jus' listenin' tuh you, Janie. Ah ain't satisfied wid mahself no mo'. Ah means tuh make Sam take me fishin' wid him after this" (284). Moreover, Pheoby, now the sole repository of Janie's value, will protect her friend from those still mired in gender and class conflicts and intimidated by Janie's autonomy ("What she doin' coming back here in dem overhalls? Can't she find no dress to put on? . . . why don't she stay in her class" [10]). Pheoby resolves, " 'Nobody better not criticize you in mah hearin' " (284). But Janie admonishes Pheoby to take action, to move beyond confining spaces. "Pheoby, you got tuh *go* there to *know* there" (285). Just as Billie Holiday once sang about God blessing the child who's got his own, Janie intones, "Yo papa and yo' mama and nobody else can't tell yuh and show yuh. Two things everybody's got tuh do fuh theyselves. They got tuh go tuh God and they got tuh find out about livin' fuh theyselves" (285). The advice elates Pheoby all the more.

Janie's storytelling also affects the teller herself. Janie commands the house, the approaching dawn, and the horizon in ways that Kabnis with his weighty coals failed to do. Janie's house is in order, and she is aglow: "Soon everything around downstairs was shut and fastened. Janie mounted the stairs with her lamp. The light in her hand was like a spark of sun-stuff washing her face in fire. Her shadow behind fell black and headlong down the stairs. Now, in her room, the place tasted fresh again" (285). In these upper rooms—a place where one can succumb to a lonely, silent death from heartbreak, as does Morrison's Sula (see Chapter 6)—Janie is joined by the singing spirit of Tea Cake, who "came prancing around her where she was and the song of the sigh flew out of the window and lit in the top of the pine trees. . . . He could never be dead until she herself had finished feeling and thinking" (286). Janie's last gesture merges love with landscape: "She pulled in her horizon like a great fish-net." And she makes that broad gesture a concrete measure of her control, "Pulled it from around the waist of the world and draped it over her shoulder" (286). This successful gesture is due to Janie's complete passage through the geography of her cultural past and the hilly terrains in her marriages, which brings Janie close to nature.

As a young girl Janie observed nature in its beauty and sexuality through the activity of bees and pear blossoms in Nanny's yard. Her discovery of love in nature and the nature of love prepares her to experience their duality in life: love can be uplifting or heartbreaking, and nature can be life-affirming or life-threatening. Nanny learned this lesson as a fugitive slave during her flight into the woods. Nanny's escape and Janie's later trek through hurricane and flood offer significant parallels. Janie encounters the same harsh "wilderness," yet she perceives an irony about landscape that had eluded

Nanny's vigilance: the lowlands can be high ground. Paradoxically, Janie comes to this awareness only by rebelling against Nanny: "Here Nanny had taken the biggest thing God ever made, the horizon . . . and pinched it in to such a little bit of a thing that she could tie it about her granddaughter's neck tight enough to choke her. She hated the old woman who had twisted her so in the name of love" (138). When Janie reaches high ground away from the flood and later in the upper rooms of her house, the horizon is no longer tied about her neck, but draped with authority around her shoulders.

Nanny, however, was not all wrong. The security and protection she wanted for Janie were merely metaphors of self-possession and autonomy. Nanny did not want Janie jumping from "pillar tuh post" (31), drifting like her daughter, Leafy, nor did Nanny want Janie to have to "tuk [her] head," or to crumple her feathers "by folks throwin' up things in [her] face," or to let men make a "spit-cup" out of her (37). However, Nanny was unaware of the subtle ways in which even socially promising marriages can wreak the same harm: Killicks made Janie into a spit-cup by asking her to do some of the most degrading farmwork (moving a manure pile) and to plow behind a mule, which put Janie close to becoming the mule Nanny had warned about. Jody went so far as to make Janie tuck her hair under a kerchief ("her hair was NOT going to show in the store"). Only the landless, penniless Tea Cake—an adult version of the adolescent Johnny Taylor—helped Janie to unfurl hair and feathers in their equitable relationship. Hurston's language demonstrates the equality; her sentences balance compound subjects engaged in a single action: "Tea Cake and Janie gone hunting. Tea Cake and Janie gone fishing. Tea Cake and Janie gone to Orlando to the movies. Tea Cake and Janie gone to a dance. . . . Tea Cake and Janie playing checkers; playing coon-can; playing Florida flip on the store porch all afternoon as if nobody else was there" (166–67).

This passage compares well with a similar moment of active transformation in Toni Morrison's novel *Song of Solomon* when Milkman ceases exploiting women and becomes responsible for reciprocal sharing in his relationship with Sweet. Here, too, the sentences reflect equilibrium: "He soaped and rubbed her until her skin squeaked and glistened like onyx. She put salve on his face. He washed her hair. She sprinkled talcum on his feet. He straddled her behind and massaged her back. She put witch hazel on his swollen neck. He made up the bed. She gave him gumbo to eat. He washed the dishes. She washed his clothes and hung them out to dry. He scoured her tub" (285). Both writers view sharing as essential to the maturation and self-possession of their protagonists. Janie's equalizing relationship with Tea Cake helps her to acquire full possession of herself and her landscape. Pheoby notices this rejuvenating transformation and says to Janie, "You looks like you'se yo' own daughter" (14). Janie has created herself.

Janie's increasing autonomy leads her to command terrestrial paths to the horizon, to conquer territories usually associated with men, and to survive nature in its harshest form. The women in her family serve as guides. Nanny, when a slave, took refuge in the woods with Leafy (aptly named). As an adolescent, Leafy was raped and hidden in the woods until she dragged herself out "on her hands and knees" (36). To save Janie from similar rude encounters with men, with the wilds, and with untamed sexuality, and to prevent Janie's head from tucking or her feathers from crumpling, Nanny acquired her own territory; she "raked and scraped and bought dis lil' piece uh land" (37). Janie learns that deliverance from the wilderness and an embrace of the horizon must be earned. Janie tells Pheoby, "you got tuh *go* there to *know* there" (285). Janie effects her "deliverance" by exercising her autonomy audaciously. She changes ordinary regions of sexist restrictions into womanist places of control. These spaces include the road, the porch, the muck, and the porch again. Things do come around in queer ways.

The road by Nanny's gatepost, for example, is where Janie allowed herself to be kissed by Johnny Taylor. The road suggests the probability of change and movement in life. During her first marriage, Janie discovers a truth about Logan Killicks's sixty acres "on de big road" (41): it is a kind of wilderness, "a lonesome place like a stump in de middle of the woods where nobody had ever been. The house was absent of flavor, too" (39). Janie remembers to keep alert by the road, and soon she hears Jody's whistling. The road is public and exists outside the authority of Nanny or Killicks, and it becomes a womanist area when Janie assertively (womanishly) rushes to the pump and deliberately attracts Jody's attention by drawing water noisily and letting "her heavy hair fall down" (47). Janie is poised for the adventure she discerns in Jody's "citified, stylish" manner, in his aura of confidence.

Janie travels the road with Jody away from Killicks's fields and in a manner indicating her new life: riding in the high chair of Jody's rented carriage. Together they arrive at a settlement, which is nothing more than a "raw place in de woods" (56). Jody will attempt to tame this wilderness of sorts by civic cultivation (as opposed to Killicks's skill in farm cultivation); he aspires to "sitting on high" as the town's mayor with Janie presiding silently over the porch. "A pretty doll-baby lak you is made to sit on de front porch and rock and fan yo'self and eat p'taters dat other folks plant just special for you" (49). The road Jody follows leads him to a false social elevation and an exploitative superiority. The more honest uplift for Janie occurs with Tea Cake, whose real name, Vergible Woods, suggests an important homonym for "veritable" or "authentic" and a kind of wilds that eludes the superficial cultivation of farm or town. Indeed, Tea Cake enters the novel by an access road leading *from* the Dixie Highway (the reverse of the detour that got Leafy "lost"). The lovers then take more indirect routes to the muck.

Roads to the muck and through the Everglades fill Janie with excitement. She is struck by the sheer exuberance of life and the outrageous fertile wildness of the countryside, untameable by mules or mayors: "Big Lake Okechobee, big beans, big cane, big weeds, big everything. Weeds that did well to grow waist high up the state were eight and often ten feet tall down there. Ground so rich that everything went wild. Volunteer cane just taking the place. Dirt roads so rich and black that a half mile of it would have fertilized a Kansas wheat field. Wild cane on either side of the road hiding the rest of the world. People wild too" (193). In Eatonville, the road leads to the porch and back to the road. The proximity of both enables Janie to seize opportunities for risk-taking and self-creation. She womanizes the spaces, transforms them from gender-imposed prisons into freedom-granting environments. In so doing she reverses familiar stereotypes associating men with the abandon of the road and women with the stationary, confining domesticity of the house.

Structurally, the porch is the part of a dwelling that mediates between the road, full of unpredictable situations, characters, events, and public occasions, and the house, where intimate family relations and events take place. The porch is the intermediary between public and private spaces and selves; thus it shares aspects of each: neighbors or passers-by visit or congregate on the porch, and family gatherings or disputes may flow onto the porch and attract attention. Jody's porch is an extension of the store he owns, and it becomes a gathering place for the town, mostly the men. It is also the place where oral lore is created spontaneously when "picture talkers" and "muletalkers" and "gum grease[rs]" (85) exercise their verbal talent. Jody prohibits Janie from joining in the fun: "mah wife don't know nothin' 'bout no speech-makin'. . . . She's uh woman and her place is in de home" (69). Jody's attempt to consolidate all authority in himself as the only big voice in town ends up silencing Janie and reducing her to the level of a possession ("yo' belov-ed wife, yo' store, yo' land," observes a neighbor [67]). Jody recognizes Janie only as an extension of himself (his porch). His big voice "makes uh big woman outa you" (74), he tells her. Jody fails to see the consequences attending his ambivalent treatment of Janie; he elevates her out of reach of the community only to reduce her to an object. The false elitism in his having erected "a high chair" for Janie "to sit in and overlook the world" (98) eludes him.

As the town increases in population, prosperity, and sophistication, Janie is further dehumanized. Indeed, the community is created at the expense of Janie's lack of participation in it. Jody's patronizing attitude does little to hide his real thinking: "Somebody got to think for women and chillun and chickens and cows" (110)—a grim reminder of Frederick Douglass's comment about male and female slaves customarily lined up and inventoried along with plantation livestock. Jody is unaware of the danger in his isolation of Janie, who is made to sit on the porch with her hair tucked in (thus becoming his porch) and denied participation in the checker playing, the taletelling, playing the dozens, or merely enjoying good, rousing conversation. When Jody oversteps his own boundary and remarks about Janie's age, "You ain't no young courtin' gal," threatening to diminish her feminine guile, Janie gets the better of him with a more damaging insult. In front of his porch cronies Janie belittles his virility: "Talkin' 'bout *me* lookin' old! When you pull down yo' britches, you look lak de change uh life" (122, 123). Jody is exposed in that vulnerable place of the porch, where public and private worlds intersect and where Janie later on becomes the victim of gossip and speculation.

Janie challenges the authority of the porch again at the novel's close when she saunters by the town gossips in her overalls. Janie's proud walk *past* the porches of her offended neighbors ("She could stop and say a few words with us" [12]) shows her triumph over the restricting space and her new measure of autonomy. Janie transforms and personalizes the porch into a "womanist" liberating environment by washing her road weary feet there. She makes the porch into a stage for self-creation by telling (performing) her tale to Pheoby. Her performance and Pheoby's transmission of Janie's tale to others will ensure Janie's authority in the house and on the porch. Janie's initial step away from Jody's porch also completed her break from Nanny's literal geography of social uplift and Janie's embrace of Tea Cake's symbolic geography of personal recovery. On the muck there were no porches. Janie tells Pheoby, " 'Ah done lived Grandma's way, now Ah means tuh live mine'" (171). Furthermore: "'Sittin' on porches lak de white madam looked lak uh mighty fine thing tuh her. Dat's whut she wanted for me—don't keer whut it cost. Git up on uh high chair and sit dere. She didn't have time tuh think whut tuh do after you got up on de stool uh do nothin'. De object wuz tuh git dere. So Ah got up on de high stool lak she told me, but Pheoby, Ah done nearly languished tuh death up dere. Ah felt like de world wuz cryin' extry and Ah ain't read de common news yet'" (172).

With Tea Cake Janie learns to read the common news; she starts to speak the "maiden language" all over again; she learns to play checkers; she listens to him at her piano, "playing blues and singing, and throwing grins over his shoulder" (156). She also follows Tea Cake to the muck, the source of his language and music and the turning point for her identity: "Blues made and used right on the spot. Dancing, fighting, singing, crying, laughing, winning and losing love every hour. . . . The rich black earth clinging to bodies and biting the skin like ants" (197). This social chaos makes the wilderness all the more redeeming.

On the muck Janie regains the voice Jody had crowded out of her. Among the common bean pickers and "people ugly from ignorance and broken from being poor" (196), Janie acquires the skills denied her previously. Although the cultural life on the muck is similar to that in Eatonville, Janie is encouraged this time to participate: "The men held big arguments here like they used to do on the store porch. Only here, she could listen and laugh and even talk some herself if she wanted to. She got so she could tell big stories herself from listening to the rest. Because she loved to hear it, and the men loved to hear themselves, they would 'woof' and 'boogerboo' around the games to the limit" (200). These skills of self-reliance and social interaction immerse Janie in the folk culture and prepare her to confront the flooding of the Okechobee lake during a hurricane. Nature puts Janie's abilities and her autonomy to a harsh test.

When Tea Cake, Motor Boat, and Janie willfully and audaciously ignore nature's warnings about the impending bad weather (the retreating Indians, the animals leaving the lowlands for high ground), they become "three fugitives" against the screaming wind and high water. "The sea was walking the earth with a heavy heel" (239). With their eyes watching God, Janie and Tea Cake earn their deliverance by engaging the flood in which the former places of Janie's confinement appear overturned ("Houses without roofs, and roofs without houses" [251]). Tea Cake and Janie save each other from drowning, but Tea Cake succumbs to rabies. Here Janie must have the strength to defend herself against Tea Cake, and although she loses Tea Cake, she gains herself. Janie returns to Eatonville with the black earth on her overalls as proof of her new baptism. By walking past the Eatonville porches and telling Pheoby the story of her recovery, Janie reaches the high ground of self-possession Nanny had hoped for all along. Instead of preaching this sermon, Janie instructs by example. Just as Nanny had hinted, things have indeed come around in unexpected ways.

Alice Walker. "In search of my mother's garden, I found my own"

From the moment Alice Walker discovered Hurston's unmarked grave, a page in literary history was rewritten. In the often-reprinted account, originally published in *Ms.* magazine, Walker describes how she and a companion visited Eatonville; talked to Hurston's former neighbors; and found their way to an abandoned cemetery in Fort Pierce, Florida, overgrown with weeds and snakes. Following directions from the undertaker, Walker reached the center of the field of waist-high grass. She called Hurston's name several times and landed upon a rectangular depression in the ground. Walker acknowledged her kinship concretely; she raised a tombstone at the site. Saving Hurston from further sinking down, Walker closed the open circle of Hurston's career and ended Hurston's obscurity. The monument reads: "Zora Neale Hurston: 'A Genius of the South,' Novelist, Folklorist, Anthropologist, 1901–1960." The once forgotten field is now a place of remembrance, a memorial; out of a wilderness, Walker created a garden.

Walker first encountered Hurston's work while researching a story about southern folk beliefs. Hurston's two volumes of anthropological study as well as the folk sources in her fiction found Walker a willing protégée and an already proven author: "She had provided, as if she knew someday I would come along wandering in the wilderness, a nearly complete record of her life" (*In Search of Our Mothers' Gardens,* 12). Several ties exist between the two authors, not the least of which is the obvious similarity in the names of their hometowns, Eatonville and Eatonton. More important, Hurston insisted on representing the South favorably while other writers of the Harlem Renaissance, bent on assimilation, found the region an undesirable and painful reminder of segregation. Alice Walker emerged a generation later during the Black Arts Movement (roughly 1965–75) when writers favored political activism over regional culture. Walker continues to remind her readers of the rich heritage of the South. The protagonist in

Meridian (1976), Walker's second novel, laments this predicament: "Meridian alone was holding on to something the [revolutionaries] had let go. . . . But what none of them seemed to understand was that she felt herself to be, not holding on to something from the past, but *held* by something in the past: by the memory of old black men in the South . . . by the sight of young girls singing in a country choir . . . their voices the voices of angels" (14).

Walker insists on portraying the cultural underpinnings that must accompany political movements if they are to have lasting effect. Hurston and Walker, however, do not share the same political views, but Hurston's outrageous insistence on presenting the cultural richness of the South, by grounding her characters in its danger and its charm, was most influential in Walker's later works, for Hurston embraced the complexity of black life. Walker proclaims in language similar to Hurston's description of Janie's grasp of the horizon, that contradictions should be nurtured rather than neglected; they enrich us as human beings:

> Be nobody's darling;
> Be an outcast.
> Take the contradictions
> Of your life
> And wrap around
> You like a shawl,
> To parry stones
> To keep you warm.
>
> ("Be Nobody's Darling,"
> *Revolutionary Petunias,* 31)

One of those masterful contradictions is the nurturing presence of a garden, even in the midst of political violence. Sammy Lou of Rue in the title poem to Walker's second collection, *Revolutionary Petunias & Other Poems* (1973), embodies the essential complementarity between politics and culture, wilderness and garden. On her way to the electric chair for having avenged the murder of her husband by wielding a "cultivator's hoe / with verve and skill," Sammy Lou reminds her children and us as readers: " 'Don't yall forget to *water* / my purple petunias' " (29). Care for flowers is part of a ritual act of remembrance; the flowers, in their delicate contrast to the grisly murder, become living testimony to the mother, to the deed, and to control of the environment. The color purple and the petunias return regularly in Walker's work precisely because they represent nature and self-control. People plant gardens to control wilderness, to establish boundaries of human endeavor against the onslaught of nature, and to harness beauty as a exercise of taste and will. Walker's story of her mother's garden confirms this point. Her large family, kept on the move by the hardships of sharecropping, once stopped along a road long enough for her mother to gather a petunia bush, which she transplanted to beautify each subsequent residence and to stave off feelings of uprootedness and dislocation. The garden stabilized the family's sense of home, identity, and beauty in the midst of disrupting change. Recognizing these qualities in her mother's garden helped Alice Walker to cultivate her own.

Another means of control over place, geography, and self is the act of burying the dead. Here the South remains a compelling landscape despite migrations to the North or the West. Ancestry, for Walker, brings responsibility: "Forgetful of geographic resolutions as birds, / the farflung young fly South to bury / the old dead" ("Burial," 13). And unmarked graves are no reason for neglect, for graves eventually grow back into the land just as they continue to nurture the self:

> Here we have watched ten thousand
> seasons
> come and go.
> And unmarked graves atangled
> in the brush
> turn our own legs to trees
> vertical forever between earth
> and sun.
> Here we are not quick to disavow
> the pull of field and wood
> and stream;
> we are not quick to turn
> upon our dreams.
>
> ("View from Rosehill Cemetery:
> Vicksburg," 25)

Speaking in this poem not only of Mississippi, but also of the entire South, Walker acknowledges the continuity of family and history. Her three novels to date illustrate this theme with increasing success.

The Third Life of Grange Copeland (1970), Walker's first novel, shows the cycle of poverty and despair that ensnares the sharecropping family of the title character for two generations. The young Copeland, finding himself up to his neck in debt, abuses and deserts his wife Margaret. His son, Brownfield, grows up determined to lead a different life, but he is lured back into the economic dependency his father knew. Brownfield's later abuse of his wife Mem to bring her down to his level, ends in his killing her. An older Grange Copeland returns South in time to know his grandchildren. He helps to raise Ruth and provides her with money for college or whatever future she decides to pursue. This is Copeland's third life, his last chance to nurture his family and end their social isolation.

Walker's concern with land and identity appears in her choice of characters and the events that shape their lives. Grange Copeland is tied to the land in ways suggested by his name—a grange is a farmhouse or a country house, and since his poverty prevents him from owning land, he copes by sharecropping. Grange has alienated his son by his neglect, although he did observe the color of fertile soil in the infant's skin. "Sort of brownish colored fields" (178), he remarked to his wife. And she named the child accordingly and without significance: "That'll do about as well as King Albert. . . . It won't make a bit of difference what we name him" (178). But it does make a difference. Brownfield is confined as much by his mother's indifference as he is by his father's debt to the landlord, a fate Brownfield can escape no more than he can change his name. Grange's failure to nurture Brownfield, who belonged to him but whom he "never touched with his hands," preordains their common loss of authority over the land they cultivate but never own.

Brownfield's sole refuge from the cycle of sharecropping is his wife Mem, a woman whom he initially respected but now resents for her ability to read and write. When Mem has had enough of his drunkenness and wife-beating, she forces him at gunpoint to wallow in his vomit until he promises to change his behavior. This "upper" hand raises Mem above Brownfield's last bit of "manhood" and vaunted self-respect. To restore Mem's "place," Brownfield plots to bring "Miss high-'n-mighty" (107) down to his level, away from the house in town she had rented and back to a sharecropper's cabin where his earning power, however minimal, would rule. Walker criticizes the kind of male-dominated society that reduces women to mules. Her fiction allows for little of the irony attending the reversal of social roles and spatial metaphors viewed in Hurston's work. Nor is Mem's life with Brownfield a point of redeeming contact with a submerged culture as in Toomer or McKay. Only Mem's persistent gardening offers refuge and an exercise of her will over the family's frequent moves: "She hated leaving a home she'd already made and fixed up with her own hands. She hated leaving her flowers, which she always planted whenever she got her hands on flower seeds. Each time she stepped into a new place, with its new, and usually bigger rat holes, she wept. Each time she had to clean cow manure out of a room to make it habitable for her children, she looked as if she had been dealt a death blow. . . . She slogged along, ploddingly, like a cow herself, for the sake of the children. Her mildness became stupor; then her stupor became horror, desolation and, at last, hatred" (59). Mem is finally defeated by Brownfield, whose sharecropping debt to Captain Davis, like Grange's debt to Mr. Shipley, is overwhelming. Her efforts to raise her family in "four sheet-rock" rooms in town are crushed by Brownfield's preference for a "corncrib" of a barn and Mem's total submission to him.

The one character to experience some kind of enlightenment is Grange himself. Here Walker returns us to a startling view of the underground when she invites—or rather teases us with—a curious parallel to Richard Wright's legacy. Before he returns to the South, Grange sojourns among gamblers and racketeers in the North. He even thinks he has "murdered" a pregnant white woman in New York's Central Park, whom he had spied unseen from a crouched place in the woods. Grange experiences the instructive invisibility of Wright's Fred Daniels and feels as liberated by his crime as Bigger Thomas did in *Native Son,* whom Walker disparagingly criticized for having "whitefolks on the brain" (*Mothers' Gardens,* 35). Walker toys with these parallels to show Wright's resolution to be unsatisfying, for Wright's protagonists, choosing to remain in the North, end up either as convicts about to be executed or corpses ready for the grave. Wright's characters are defeated in the North because they have allowed that environment to define them totally and to cut them off from ancestry ("I was leaving the South to fling myself into the unknown," Wright rejoices in *Black Boy*). Walker's characters remain in the South or return there (even the dreamy Brownfield, who wanted to go "Norse," never leaves). Walker's more complete revision of Wright's map of failed recovery occurs in the scene of Grange's apparent "murder" of the white woman.

Here in the North Grange has no visibility and must remind himself of his identity: "Grange. My name Grange. Grange Copeland is my name" (145). The blank stares of people look right through him as if he were not "even in existence" (144). It had been different in the South: "The South had made him miserable, with nerve endings raw from continual surveillance from contemptuous eyes, but they *knew he was there.* Their very disdain proved it. The North put him in solitary confinement where he had to manufacture his own hostile stares in order to see himself" (144–45).

One day in the park, suffering from hunger, Grange crouches "underneath" shrubbery and observes a pregnant woman being paid off and abandoned by her married lover (an act Grange himself is guilty of when he deserts Margaret). Just as Wright's Fred Daniels observed whites from his hideout in the sewers, Grange watches the woman whose despair increases to the point of her dropping the money once her lover departs. Feeling a mix of greed and pity, Grange recovers the money and tries to get the woman to share it with him. She sees him only as a "nigger," and demands all of the money. When she tries to get away from him, she falls through ice on the frozen lake. She then refuses Grange's extended hand. Grange's offer of rescue parallels Daniels's moment of compassion when he yelled "Don't" to the night watchman about to commit suicide after being accused of Daniels's crime. Both gestures by blacks to affirm mutual humanity with others, even their enemies, go unrecognized; the white woman prefers death, and she drowns *herself.* Following this accident Grange feels free from the burden of trying to make whites see him. Their death is the inevitable result of their willful blindness. Even the mounted police, oblivious to the accident, chase Grange out of Central Park, as if he had no rightful place in their "garden."

Grange's misreading of this event (he thinks he has killed the woman) makes him a false prophet of racial hatred and revenge. Unlike Daniels, who discovers a forbidden but honest truth underground and tries to communicate his knowledge, Grange brings a false message of hate to Harlem streets and storefront churches. Neither place welcomes him. "Mothers, shuffling along Lenox Avenue, with dozens of black children in tow turned to look at him with hopeless eyes" (153–54), and the churchgoers look upon him in "horrified preeminence" until the deacons put him out. Grange's zeal comes from his false righteousness: "Hatred for them will someday unite us" (154), he preaches, but his words fall on deaf ears. Unlike Daniels, he speaks no truth; the "murder" was neither real nor justifiable. The only value left to Grange is the more redeeming one of self-reliance: "But soon he realized he could not fight all the whites he met. Nor was he interested in it any longer. Each man would have to free himself, he thought, and the best way he could. For the time being, he would withdraw completely from them, find a sanctuary, make a life that need not acknowledge them, and be always prepared, with his life, to defend it, to protect it, to keep it from whites, inviolate" (155). This is why Grange returns to the South. Living his third life affirmatively, he bequeaths to Ruth the honesty and the financial means for her to secure a debt-free future with no whites on the brain.

Walker's probable "apprenticeship" under Wright is consistent with Wright's prominent place in American letters and Hurston's more unfortunate neglect. Wright presented a formidable challenge to Walker until she discovered Hurston as a more appropriate model. Walker's response to Wright is her way of breaking the cycle of negative depictions of the South and to affirm (as she does in *Meridian*) that one can "go back to the people." In her later fiction Walker celebrates not only the petunias in her mother's garden and the contradictions worn in the shawl of black life, but also a father's homage to Indian burial grounds and the neglected color purple, which must also be recognized as God's handiwork.

If *The Third Life of Grange Copeland* depicted the realistic plight of characters grounded in their limitations, mired in their weaknesses, and thus "totally without view, without a sky," then *Meridian* charts a symbolic compass of elevation. The symbolism emerges from the accumulation of definitions the author provides in a dictionary entry for "meridian" that serves as the novel's preface and the protagonist's name. The novel insists that the protagonist be measured by these definitions, from the first meaning as "the highest apparent point reached by a heavenly body in its course," to the simpler adjectival usage as "southern." The device of the dictionary entry as preface is risky, because it leads us to expect the protagonist to unify most, if not all, of these definitions. *Meridian* is a fragmentary novel about the era of the civil rights movement. The protagonist, Meridian Hill, struggles to revive community activism and civil disobedience despite the movement's decline. Traveling through small southern towns like a latter-day Harriet Tubman, Meridian works tirelessly and alone for equal rights and voter registration. Like the nameless elderly black woman in one of Walker's essays who, when asked if the movement was dead, replied: "If it's dead, it shore ain't ready to lay down" (*Mothers' Gardens,* 120), Meridian reminds us of our continuing responsibility to the movement, whether it be moribund or fragmented.

If America's failure to better race relations has ruptured society by further estranging the races, then a fragmented novel such as *Meridian* may be an accurate portrait of the times. Readers, however, are frustrated by the novel's lack of cohesion. The most readily discernible narrative thread centers around Meridian's attempt to understand conditions imposed upon her by her mother, by society, and by her friends who are members of a revolutionary group. Will she become a Christian? Will she fulfill the roles of a woman in society? Can she kill for the revolution? Unable to answer these questions affirmatively, Meridian decides to go back among the people in order to discover the nature and limits of her commitment as well as to fulfill the definitions of her name.

／When Meridian fails to embrace her mother's religion, "her mother's love was gone, withdrawn, and there were conditions to be met before it would be returned" (17).／When she refuses to reject the past the revolutionaries abandoned, "they made her ashamed of that past, and yet all of them shared it. The church, the music" (17). When her wavering continues and her friend Anne-Marion asks, "Then will you kill for the Revolution, not just die for it?" Meridian remains honestly uncertain: "I don't know." The group turns away from her, and Meridian turns back to the people: "I'll go back to the people, live among them, like Civil Rights workers used to do" (18). This pivotal moment in Meridian's life merges her identity with the geographical meaning of her name, "a great circle of the earth passing through the geographical poles and any given point on the earth's surface" (1). Meridian progresses throughout the novel to become the highest "point of prosperity, splendor, power" that the revolutionaries advocate, but she alone achieves.

In addition to the North-South geographical poles represented by a host of characters (white civil rights workers from northern colleges, such as Lynne Rabinowitz and the pretentious black Francophile, Truman Held, who becomes Meridian's boyfriend but marries Lynne), the novel posits two poles of political tactics: the violence advocated by the revolutionary group ("I know violence *is* as American as cherry pie!" [18] Meridian admits) and the nonviolence of the civil rights movement, which "has failed" to change the system. Meridian moves between these extremes. She returns to the South to work among the people as a teacher, dishwasher, gardener, all to recover the humanitarian spirit the revolutionaries have forgotten. Meridian aims "to see them, to be with them, to understand them and herself, the people who now fed her and tolerated her and also, in a fashion, cared about her" (19).

Just as Meridian turns to the people, the novel turns to Meridian's life, depicting her growing up in the South, her alienation from her family, and her involvement with the early civil rights protests. At one demonstration she is beaten by police, and she continues to suffer from unexpected dizziness and occasional paralysis. On her return South, Meridian becomes more of a Harriet Tubman figure. Dressed in overalls and a railroad cap over her thinning hair, she leads small protests to keep the movement alive. In tiny southern towns neglected by protestors in favor of larger cities, Meridian's efforts amount to small miracles. Like Hurston's Janie Starks, Meridian learns to read the "common news." She refuses the circumscribed roles that the revolutionary group and conventional society have assigned to her. In the process she loses Truman Held to Lynne but not her *hold* on him, nor her hold on the real pulse of the people.

These fragments of plot and character point to a submerged wholeness in the novel, which may have only a surface fragmentation. Yet those arcs of irresolution from *Cane* threaten to reappear, for meridian also means a "half circle." One unifying element may be the curious event that opens the novel. Meridian leads a group of poor black children to see a traveling freak show to which they have been denied admission on any but the day set aside for them and at a higher ticket price. Meridian stares down a menacing army tank and takes the children to see the mummified white woman on view. The corpse has been dragged from town to town by the penitent husband who had killed her in a jealous rage. "Marilyn O'Shay" is presented as a object lesson and freak, and her "crime" is spelled out: "Obedient Daughter," "Devoted Wife," "Adoring Mother," "Gone Wrong" (5). Although everyone, including the children, knows the mummy is a fake, the real interest lies in the public "punishment" of a woman who was not content to "lay back and be pleasured" (6). The accusation of fakery has dual significance: the mummy is a "fake" because of the artificial "embalming" and because the woman rejected the roles of a true woman, including that of Mommy.

As the novel unfolds Meridian breaks the same rules governing women's roles. She is not the obedient daughter because she refuses to join her mother's church; she is not a devoted wife because she accepts her husband's infidelity; and she is not the adoring mother because she readily gives up her son for adoption and heads off to college where she becomes involved in the civil rights movement. Later she joins a revolutionary group with her roommate Anne-Marion, who is more willing than she to hide her tenderness and respect for life under political posturing. When Meridian fails to affirm unequivocally that she would kill for the revolution, everyone all but accuses her of being a fake, of being "misguided," unwilling to "admit the truth," and "weak and insensitive to History" (10). Meridian, like the mummified corpse (or facsimile thereof), moves from town to town, proving her integrity through action. The journey diminishes her physical health, but augments her spirituality.

Meridian's travels from the South to the North and to the South again, from advocating nonviolence to considering violence and back to practicing nonviolence, become a heavenly body's orbit. Her unselfish service to the people brings her to a saintlike elevation, and her journey parallels "the highest apparent point reached by a heavenly body in its course." She reaches this elevation by going *down* among the people. Like McKay's Bita Plant, Meridian learns more from the people than she teaches them; she continues the tedious and unglamorous work of voter registration and the fight for better social services; she sings the people's songs rather than the martial tunes of the revolutionaries. When she embraces a more secular religion and attends the funeral of a slain boy, she affirms to the grieving father her willingness to kill only to protect lives: "she *would* kill, before she allowed anyone to murder his son again" (204). Yet this point is neither the beginning nor the end of Meridian's commitment; rather, it is one step in her understanding that violent defensive actions may become necessary. Meridian achieves this enlightenment long after the revolutionaries have failed to do anything concrete (Anne-Marion becomes a poet of sunsets, a mother, and a property owner). Meridian, having gone to the people, finds that, although she may not belong to the future as idealized by the revolutionaries, she can at least carry forward the past. In her acceptance of the need for violence, Meridian realizes that she, in fact, is not yet able to kill anyone. This truth is more precious to her than the "false urgings that come . . . in periods of grief and rage" (205). Meridian does not abdicate a role in history or in revolutionary struggle; she simply redefines her duty:

Perhaps it will be my part to walk behind the real revolutionaries—those who know they must spill blood in order to help the poor and the black and therefore go right ahead—and when they stop to wash off the blood and find their throats too choked with the smell of murdered flesh to sing, I will come forward and sing from memory songs they will need once more to hear. For it is the song of the people, transformed by the experiences of each generation, that holds them together, and if any part of it is lost the people suffer and are without soul. If I can only do that, my role will not have been a useless one after all. (205-6)

Her songs also redeem and transform others. Truman Held, long captivated by the superficial glamour of speaking French and marrying white, releases himself from that hold and returns to Meridian, not as a lover or husband, but as a disciple.

Truman now recognizes what he had been blind to before: the honest nature of Meridian's love, which exposed his lack of honesty and which "flowed over me," he now admits, "like a special sun, like grace" (223). Meridian moves on to other towns; Truman remains behind and continues her work. He seeks to perform the small, unglamorous "miracles" of social change. Truman dons Meridian's cap, climbs into her sleeping bag, and begins to follow her journey forward and up. He awaits the people: "Tomorrow the people would come and bring him food. Someone would come and milk his cow. They would wait patiently for him to perform, to take them along the next guideless step. Perhaps he would" (228). The meaning Meridian has discovered in her responsible rebellion may enable Truman to unleash more potential in the people and to find the fullest truth in himself and in his ancestry.

Meridian's idea of ancestry and her contagious respect for the people and their music sounds Walker's reply to LeRoi Jones's definition of the blues as masking hatred ("If Bessie Smith had killed some white people she wouldn't have needed that music"). Meridian asks simply, "If they committed murder . . . *what would the music be like?*" (15). For Walker, the people's music transforms rather than represses hatred; it engenders self-recognition. The songs Meridian sings come from the voice of history. *The Color Purple* (1982), Walker's third novel, examines this theme further and moves away from the public sphere of political movements and into the private world of the family where sexual harassment and marital abuse inhibit self-recognition and fulfillment. Whereas *Meridian* documented the arc of travel from alternate geographical poles and states of political consciousness, *The Color Purple* uses landscape imagery to depict passage from the bruise to the beauty of purple in one woman's journey to song and self-possession.

Walker's text, the only epistolary novel to date in Afro-American literature, explores the lives of two sisters, Celie and Nettie, who are abused by their stepfather, Pa, and by Celie's husband, Albert. Celie is raped by Pa and has two children, whom Pa sells to a local minister. Celie is later given in marriage to Albert as if she were property. Albert prefers the younger, more attractive Nettie. Celie protects Nettie and encourages her to run away to the minister. Albert, in a rage, prevents any further communication between the sisters by intercepting the letters each writes. Nettie ends up raising

Celie's children in the minister's family, and they embark for Liberia to work as missionaries among the Olinka people. Celie, meanwhile, knows nothing of their whereabouts. Through the relationship Celie forms with a woman blues singer, Shug Avery, she discovers how to end her isolation and recover a sense of herself. Fascinating in its rendering of black speech as Celie gropes toward articulation about her feelings and her life, the novel also shows that estrangement and great geographical distances do not free the sisters from male or tribal oppression. The lives of the Olinka women in Liberia are just as prescribed as Celie's in the rural South, yet Celie, "pore and black and ugly," is the most foreign, abused, and dejected. She travels the farthest journey from such low self-esteem to such self-possession that readers find themselves rejoicing with her.

The multiple denotative and connotative meanings for purple in the novel follow Walker's now familiar trend of creating new terms, such as "womanist," and redefining others, such as meridian. Celie becomes disfigured by the purple bruises of rape, of childbearing while still a child herself (which brings on sterility), and of life as a battered wife. She matures into a woman who wears purple pants with a dignity befitting her newly found beauty. Purple signals this transformation, but Walker lodges the change in an abiding respect for cultivated landscapes: gardens.

Entrapped in a rural field, far from society, and held almost captive in a wilderness of abuse heaped on her by stepfather, husband, and stepchildren, Celie loses almost all sense of who she is. The first letter (written to God) indicates the decline in Celie's self-perception when she revises the opening lines: "I am I have always been a good girl." This initial change and uncertainty turn to self-negation when Celie is made to satisfy Pa's sexual needs and when her children are taken away from her. The roles of "Obedient Daughter," "Dutiful Wife," and "Adoring Mother," mocked in *Meridian,* are systematically denied Celie until she is dehumanized and internalizes negation. No longer able to have children, she becomes no more than a field hand ("She can work like a man," Pa tells Albert), and she comes to the arranged marriage (principally to take care of Albert's children) with her own linen and livestock: "She can take that cow she raise down there back of the crib" (10), Pa offers to sweeten the deal.

When Celie first hears about the blues singer Shug Avery, the disreputable lover Albert was not man enough to marry over his father's objections, and when Celie first sees her photograph, she imagines Shug to be royalty, a Queen Honeybee. Buying material for the dress she will be the first to wear,

Celie emulates Shug by seeking purple fabric: "I think what color Shug Avery would wear. She like a queen to me, so I say to Kate, Somethin purple, maybe little red in it too. But us look an look and no purple" (20). Although Celie must settle for a different hue, she will eventually have the color purple and Shug herself as friend, confidante, and lover. Their relationship becomes the means for Celie to discover her own beauty.

Before meeting Shug, Celie had protected herself from further abuse from men by making herself wooden. "It all I can do not to cry," Celie reports after a beating by Albert. "I make myself wood. I say to myself, Celie, you a tree. That's how come I know trees fear man" (22). Celie wills herself into a state of rigid verticality in order to shield herself from pain. Celie believes she is ugly. As a tree, she so merges with the wilderness of unbridled sexuality and brutality that she mistakenly advises her stepson Harpo to beat his disobedient wife. When a distraught Albert brings Shug to the house after she had collapsed during a singing engagement, Shug sees Celie as an element of the wild field and chaotic household. As Shug begins to recuperate under Celie's care and Albert's undiminished affection, she connects Celie with nature in which the color purple—God's handiwork— goes unrecognized and disrespected. Celie as a child of God (indeed His faithful correspondent) is the neglected blossom, a revolutionary petunia in disguise, which Shug, like the children of Sammy Lou of Rue, must nurture. It is Shug who makes the vital connection between Celie and the novel's title: "I think it pisses God off if you walk by the color purple in a field somewhere and don't notice it" (167). By her notice, Shug draws Celie out of her woodenness, out of the field or wilderness where she had been abandoned.

Shug also helps Celie to see that trees and women require care. "You ever notice that trees do everything to git attention we do, except walk?" (168). And Shug insists that Celie "git man off your eyeball" (just as Grange Copeland had to get whites off the brain) to appreciate all God has made, including herself. It is not enough just to write letters to him. From this point on, Celie notices God in nature: "I been so busy thinking bout him [God as an old, white man] I never truly notice nothing God make. Not a blade of corn (how it do that?) not the color purple (where it come from?). Not the little wildflowers. Nothing" (168). Celie recovers through Shug's emotional and physical love. Shug's mediation also brings an end to Albert's beatings. To force Celie to see herself completely, Shug goes so far as to hand Celie a mirror and admonishes her to "look at yourself down there."

This new view teaches Celie how to express love for herself and love for Shug.

Shug also offers Celie the blues as a means of *ex*pression, rather than LeRoi Jones's idea of repression. If Ellison is correct in *Shadow and Act* in pointing out the autobiographical content of the blues "expressed lyrically," then Shug's gift to Celie is not only a mirror to view her body, but also a music to review her life. Shug and Celie heal each other. Celie nurses Shug back to health, and Shug helps Celie link her experiences to the larger voice of the culture in the blues. In fact, one of Shug's songs is called "Miss Celie's song," Shug announces, because "she scratched it out of my head when I was sick" (65).

The blues here is redemptive. Just as Tea Cake rescued Janie Starks by his blues singing and by taking her to the geographical source of the music, the muck (or, as in McKay, the Ditch), Shug's music redeems Celie. Both the submerged culture and the suppressed identity resurface. This music also figures among the "old songs" Meridian sings to effect her spiritual elevation and the rise of her culture out of the wilderness of racial segregation or random violence. Although rescue and revitalization figure less in Nettie's experiences than in Celie's, Walker shows by contrast the estranged sister's similar oppression. Among the Olinka, "a girl is nothing to herself; only to her husband can she become something" (132). The women also do not look "in a man's face" (137), but at his feet or his knees. Nettie's freedom comes in her return to the South; Celie's deliverance comes in her glorious return to herself.

The return to self and to landscape is a constant theme in Alice Walker's fiction and essays. But the subject of recovery has been the concern of many black women writers who seek various kinds of redemption for women who have been imprisoned in sexist fantasy or racist stereotype for too long. Gayl Jones offers her meditation on this theme through her exercise of a language destined to give evidence of how women have prevailed over adversity. Jones's protagonist, the blues singer Ursa Corregidora, attempts to achieve justice and reconciliation in her accusatory songs in which two spatial metaphors predominate: the terrestrial image of a tunnel closing about a train and the celestial image of a bird-woman taking a man away on a journey and never bringing him back. In Jones's sexual geography, the field is rocky and mined with acts of mutual abuse.

In contrast to Walker's embrace of open spaces to help achieve kinship with others and recognition of self (the trance both Meridian and her father experience atop an Indian burial mound, and Walker's own homage to marked and unmarked graves), Gayl Jones explores the interior habitations of generational responsibility. Again, Walker's notion of "womanist" is useful as a way of contrasting Jones's two main protagonists. Whereas Ursa Corregidora learns to exert her will and outrageous voice over the residual history haunting her songs, Eva Medina Canada embraces a psychological silence and capitulates to male definitions of her place and personality. Her voice sounds nothing more than a terrifying one-syllable cry.

Gayl Jones. "Singing a Deep Song." Language as Evidence and Landscape

Since the publication of her first novel, *Corregidora* (1975), Gayl Jones has figured among the best contemporary Afro-American writers who have used black speech as a major aesthetic device in their works. Like Alice Walker and Toni Morrison, Jones uses the rhythm and structure of spoken language to establish the authenticity of her characters and to create new possibilities for conflict within the text and between readers and the text itself. Rather than merely introducing readers to the culture, she totally immerses us in the landscape of racial and sexual idiom, where corrective, retributive behavior halts a generational pattern of sexual abuse and restores human dignity.

> The blues calling my name.
> She is singing a deep song.
> She is singing a deep song.
> I am human.
>
> ("Deep Song," *Chant
> of Saints*, 376)

Redemption most likely occurs when the resolution of conflict is forged in the same vocabulary as the tensions that precipitated it. This dual nature of language makes it appear brutally indifferent, for it contains the source and the solution of conflict. Yet language is the main evidence writers have to offer in their appeal for justice, human and cosmic. Jones's fictional landscape is the relationship between men and women, a field her characters mine with dishonesty, manipulation, and mutual abuse. The battleground is sex, and Jones uses the right sexual vocabulary to conduct the strategy of the war. Results vary; it can be the ambiguous yet healing reconciliation of a blues stanza shared between Mutt and Ursa in *Corregidora,* or a lonely woman's solo cry at orgasm in *Eva's Man.* What Jones is after are the words and deeds that finally break the sexual bondage men and women impose upon each other. When language is drawn from the musical and sexual idiom and shared with the reader or between characters in a ritualistic cadence of speech rendered like a song or an incantation, there is a chance that painful wounds may be healed. Such reconciliation is possible through an evidence of words spoken, sung, communicated. Acts of language can be regenerative: predatory characters can recover their briefly lost selves by reconnecting to the textures of love and identity in black American speech.

Afro-American language and storytelling tradition are the main sources of Jones's development as a writer. "I used to say that I learned to write by listening to people talk," she told one interviewer. "I still feel that the best of my writing comes from having *heard* rather than having read. . . . My first stories were heard stories—from grown-up people talking" (*Chant,* 352). The oral tradition creates an immediate community for the teller and the listener, a situation Jones recreates in fiction to get inside the story, to bridge the gap between writer and reader and to establish reciprocal communication. This close relationship preserves and nourishes tradition: "When you tell a story, you automatically talk about traditions, but they're never separate from the people, the human implications. You're talking about language, you're talking about politics and morality and economics and culture. . . . You're talking about all your connections as a human being" (353).

The discernible "literary" influences in Jones's fiction come from writers in the orally based cultures of some Native American groups and those of Africa, Europe, and Latin America; from N. Scott Momaday and Amos Tutuola to Chaucer, James Joyce, and Carlos Fuentes. The oral features in the work of these writers make the act of hearing an important element of their craft. "Hearing has to be essential," says Jones. "You have to be able to hear other people's voices and you have to be able to hear your own voice." In her own work she admits, "I have to bring the written things into the oral *mode* before I can *deal with* them" (354–55).

The distinctive feature in Jones's fiction is not its faithful transcription of ordinary speech, but the transformation of that speech into "ritualized dialogue," which alters "the rhythm of the talk and the response." Readers encounter at least three levels of linguistic activity: "the language, the rhythm of the people talking, and the rhythm *between* the people talking." Language is ritualized to find meaning in the musicality of speech and to explore its capacity to convey themes. The quality of language is enriched: "You change the rhythm of the talk and response and you change the rhythm *between* the talk and response. So in ritualized dialogue, you do something to the rhythm or you do something to the words. You change the kinds of words they would use or the rhythm of those words. But both things take the dialogue out of the naturalistic realm—change its quality" (359). Readers find themselves in much the same role of active listener as the writer herself has been. The transformation of oral into written expression (we are in fact *reading* the text) requires a new appreciation of the figurative and ritualistic levels of meaning in speech.

Moreover, spoken language rendered in dialogue or in narration in Jones's fiction allows us to examine character and theme from a different angle: the character's diction and attitude toward words and deeds facilitates or hinders reconciliation, which is the underlying goal of Jones's characters. Richly drawn and complex, the characters and voices of Ursa Corregidora and Eva Medina Canada create a landscape of language as their witness to the place of justice and redemption in love—a goal only one of them achieves.

"Corregidor*e*," from the Portuguese, means "a former judicial magistrate." By changing the gender designation, Jones makes Ursa Corregidora a female judge charged by the women in her family to "correct" the historical invisibility they have suffered, "to give evidence" of their abuse, and "to make generations" as a defense against their further displacement and annihilation. Ursa's name also comes from the man responsible for much of this pain, the Brazilian coffee planter and whoremaster, Corregidora. Ursa must bring justice to bear upon his past exploitation of blacks as slaves and women as whores and upon his haunting contamination of her present life.

Corregidora opens with an act of violence: Mutt Thomas in a jealous rage knocks Ursa, his recently pregnant wife and a blues singer, down a flight of stairs. Hospitalized, Ursa loses her child and womb and can never fulfill the pledge made by the women in her family "to make generations." The novel details Ursa's attempt to free herself from guilt imposed by her physical limitation and from resentment against her now estranged husband. Mutt, however, is not the sole culprit. Ursa learns that she comes from generations of abused women and women abusers. Great Gram was the slave and concubine of Corregidora. Their child became his mistress and bore another woman, Ursa's mother. When "papers" were burned to deny that slavery ever existed, that these women may not have ever existed, their only defense lay in making generations to preserve the family. As Ursa has been admonished to do from the time she was five: *"Because they didn't want to leave no evidence of what they done—so it couldn't be held against them. And I'm leaving evidence. And you got to leave evidence. And your children got to leave evidence. And when it come time to hold up the evidence, we got to have evidence to hold up. That's why they burned all the papers, so there wouldn't be no evidence to hold up against them"* (14). This oral pledge must accomplish what the written record no longer can.

The pledge not only binds Ursa to procreation, but it also revives in her mind the cruel specter of Corregidora himself. When Ursa is abused by Mutt and forced to come to new terms with her femininity, the images of Corregidora and Mutt merge, and she feels abused by both simultaneously. Mutt, however, has attacked Ursa without knowing she was pregnant. He makes it impossible for her to "give evidence" through making generations, and she must find another way. Indirectly, Mutt has made it possible for Ursa to free herself from the pattern of *mutual* abuse implicit in the pledge itself. Ursa, haunted by the relationship between Great Gram and Corregidora, learns that she was about to continue the oppressive matrilinearity that held men and women captive to the need for generations in the manner preordained by her foremothers:

> Because I realized for the first time I had what those women had. I'd always thought I was different. *Their* daughter, but somehow different. Maybe less Corregidora. I don't know. But when I saw that picture, I knew I had it. What my mother and my mother's mother before her had. The mulatto women. Great Gram was the coffee-bean woman, but the rest of us... But I *am* different now, I was thinking. I have everything they had, except the generations. I can't make generations. And even if I still had my womb, even if the first baby *had* come—what would I have done then? Would I have kept it up? Would I have been like *her*, or *them?* (60)

Mutt's deed forces Ursa to come to new terms, new language about her personal and generational identity. The different way Ursa learns to give evidence is by singing the blues in what she suspects is a "new voice" following her recuperation. She is then prepared to confront her past and conquer it as best she can.

At the end of the novel and after a separation of twenty-two years—the narrative's only strain on credibility—Ursa reunites with Mutt. She is no longer a passive victim of abuse nor is she a solo blues singer. Ursa avenges herself on Mutt by performing fellatio on him—an act that places her in control of herself and Mutt. Ursa exchanges her role as a blues singer whose mouth contains "a hard voice," a voice that "hurts you and makes you still want to listen," into an instrument of direct sexual power: "What is it a woman can do to a man that make him hate her so bad he wont to kill her one minute and keep thinking about her and can't get her out of his mind the next?" The rhetorical question is meant to bridge historical time and place, to unite Ursa's present coupling with Mutt to the act between Great Gram and Corregidora. "It had to be sexual," Ursa thinks, "it had to be something sexual that Great Gram did to Corregidora. . . . In a split second I knew what it was, in a split second of hate and love I knew what it was. . . . A moment of pleasure and excruciating pain at the same time . . . a moment that stops before it breaks the skin: 'I could kill you' " (184). Mutt and Ursa are in the same Drake Hotel where they spent the early days of their marriage. "It wasn't the same room, but the same place. The same feel of the place. I knew what he wanted. I wanted it too. We didn't speak. We got out of our clothes. I got between his knees" (184). The return to their own past simultaneously returns them to the past of the initial tension and conflict between Ursa's ancestors: "It was like I didn't know how much was me and Mutt and how much was Great Gram and Corregidora" (184). This metaphorical return allows Ursa to go forward; her reconciliation with Mutt is achieved through sex and a ritualized dialogue that assumes the rhythm, structure, and tone of a blues stanza:

> "I don't want a kind of woman that hurt you," he said.
> "Then you don't want me."
> "I don't want a kind of woman that hurt you."
> "Then you don't want me."
> "I don't want a kind of woman that hurt you."
> "Then you don't want me."

The blues language is evidence for the *re* generation Ursa and Mutt experience: "He shook me till I fell against him crying. 'I don't want a kind of man that'll hurt me neither,' I said. He held me tight" (185).

Furthermore, the six line call-response pattern above reflects the blues structure of the novel itself and the pattern of Ursa's developing consciousness. The narrative is shaped by the three-part incremental repetition of storyline from Great Gram to Gram, Gram to Mama, Mama to Ursa: "My great-grandmama told my grandmama the part she lived through that my grandmama didn't live through and my grandmama told my mama what they both lived through and my mama told me what they all lived through and we were suppose to pass it down like that from generation to generation so we'd never forget. Even though they'd burned everything to play like it didn't never happen" (9). Ursa sings a different song. And like the last line in most blues stanzas, her new words resolve the song's narrative, but only after she reunites with Mutt.

Corregidora, immortalized in the oral history, is husband to all the women, including Mama who, although she married Martin and later separated from him, kept her maiden name. Corregidora also threatens to possess Ursa until Mutt's jealous rage frees her from the grip of those generations. During the years of her estrangement from Mutt, Ursa grows aware of mutual abuse and the danger of her potential acquiescence "like Mama when she started talking like Great Gram" (184). The knowledge Ursa gains that leads her from a blues solo to the blues duet quoted above concerns the arbitrary exchange of power and the mutual consent that produces authority: "But was what Corregidora had done to *her*, to *them*, any worse than what Mutt had done to me, than what we had done to each other, than what Mama had done to Daddy, or what he had done to her in return, making her walk down the street looking like a whore?" (184). The justice Ursa finally wields comes from the fundamental ambivalence of the blues condition, what Ralph Ellison once again defined as an "autobiographical chronicle of personal *catastrophe* expressed *lyrically*" (79, emphasis mine); from language comes control, a form to contain and transmit experience.

Mutt, although inarticulate about his deepest feelings and love for Ursa, understands her dilemma. His jealousy is justifiable, on the one hand, because he regards Corregidora as a rival for Ursa's attention, indeed *love;* on the other hand, he feels ensnared in the abusive stereotype of a male breeder, a role Martin rejected when he realized the conspiracy of the elder Corregidora women against him. Mutt was drawn to Ursa by the bewitching power of her songs. Ursa's voice, like that of a black siren, lures men to a potentially tragic fate. But Ursa is also trapped in the act of luring men. In this regard she bears strong resemblance to Lula in LeRoi Jones's *Dutchman,* who never finds her way *out* of the underground subway. Ursa is similarly trapped in history, but she finds her way to safety by learning the truth of her mother's marriage and by reuniting with Mutt. Feeling that he knows Ursa "from way back," Mutt is both her opponent and friend, largely from what he intuits from the evidence of her songs and their menacing landscapes: "When I first saw Mutt I was singing a song about a train tunnel. About this train going in the tunnel, but it didn't seem like they was no end to the tunnel, and nobody knew when the train would get out, and then all of a sudden the tunnel tightened around the train like a fist. Then I sang about this bird woman, whose eyes were deep wells. How she would take a man on a long journey, but never return him" (147). Ursa's attraction to Mutt makes him an audience of one: "he got to be the man I was singing to. I would look at him when I began a song and somehow I would be looking at him when I ended it" (148). Mistaking him for all men, Ursa is slow to appreciate Mutt's individuality or his ability to help her escape the oppressive hold of Corregidora. Ursa is also guilty of trying to fit Mutt into Corregidora's role, and not opening up to him or letting the tunnel release the train trapped underground:

> When I'd flared back at him with his own kind of words, he'd say, "You never used to talk like that. How'd you get to talk like that?"
>
> I answered, "I guess you taught me. Corregidora taught Great Gram to talk the way she did."
>
> "Don't give me hell, Ursa," he said now. "You know this is hell. Don't you feel anything? Don't you want me?"
>
> "Yes," I said.
>
> "I want to help you, but I can't help you unless you help me."
>
> He had parted my legs, but I pushed him away. (152–53)

Mutt tries to tell Ursa that she isn't the hard woman she thinks she must be, but she persists in wearing the mask. Later, he refuses Ursa sex in retaliation for her use and abuse of him. Mutt's last act of aggression, knocking Ursa accidentally down a flight of stairs, breaks their dual tie to Corregidora: Ursa's womb.

The loss of her womb precipitates Ursa's journey back into the past to recover a female identity lost with her inability to make generations, the main source of identity for her foremothers. On the way Ursa rejects the lesbian advances of Cat Lawson and Jeffey, and has a brief marriage with Tadpole, a bar owner who also tries to help Ursa feel like a woman again.

But the only people who can help are her mother and Mutt, leading her right back to the sexual geography of the past and to a new level of struggle with Corregidora.

When Ursa takes the initiative to visit her mother and urges her to talk, she learns how Mama was virtually made into a whore not by Martin, but by Great Gram and Gram, who needed generations to continue their rage against Corregidora more than they needed men as stable family partners. "They'd tell me, they'd be telling me," Mama says, "about making generations, but I wasn't out looking for no man. I never was out looking for no man. I kept thinking back on it, though, and it was like I had to go there, had to go there and sit there and have him watch me like that. . . . You know how mens watch you when they wont something" (112). This is the same look Mutt accuses Ursa of seeking: "If you wasn't one of them you wouldn't like them mens watching after you." But by the time Ursa's mother met Martin, she was already trapped: "Like my body or something knew what it wanted even if I didn't want no man. Cause I knew I wasn't looking for none. But it was like it knew it wanted you. It was like my whole body knew it wanted you and knew it would have you, and knew you'd be a girl" (114). The unnamed force here is Corregidora.

Martin's discovery that he was simply the surrogate breeder for Corregidora causes the breakup of the marriage. Martin tells Mama, "Shit. Money's not how I helped you. I helped you that night didn't I? . . . I lived in that house long enough to know I helped you. How long was it? Almost two years, wasn't it? That's long enough for any man to know if he's helped. How could I have missed. I mean, the first time. The other times were all miss, weren't they, baby? They were all miss, weren't they?" (119). Martin then retaliates by making Mama walk through the town looking like a whore, which is what the other women were, Corregidora's whores. Mama's divorce once Ursa is born brings back the celibacy she had always preferred. She has fulfilled her pledge, and she retains her maiden name, which suggests that Mama is symbolically married to Corregidora, not Martin. Ursa also keeps her name in a sign of her dependence on Corregidora: "That's my name not my husband's." Ursa actually is about to repeat her mother's behavior, and Mutt's reaction is more perceptive than irrational: *"Ain't even took my name. You Corregidora's, ain't you? Ain't even took my name. You ain't my woman"* (61). Mutt recreates Martin's rage. Martin is not totally defeated by Corregidora or the women because he poses the one question that diminishes the moral superiority these women claimed as victims, a question even

Mama was afraid to ask: "How much was hate for Corregidora and how much was love?" (131). Martin, not Mama, had the courage to stand up against the elder women and demand they acknowledge their true feelings, admit to the ambivalence that governed their lives. Ursa's discovery of this truth frees her to return to Mutt.

Like Martin, Mutt unmasks Ursa's hardness, ambivalence, enslavement to Corregidora's history, and lack of identity (although Ursa is on the way to recovering her identity after the visit to Mama). *"Forget what they went through,"* Mutt pleads with Ursa, who confesses: *"I can't forget. The space between my thighs. A well that never bleeds"* (99). And, *"I never told you how it was. Always their memories, but never my own"* (100). Ursa gains her own memory and identity once she hears Mama's story and realizes that her blues singing, meant to give evidence and witness (*"They squeezed Corregidora into me, and I sung back in return"* [103]), only bound her tighter to the past. What she must now articulate is not language itself, but the rhythm *between* people talking, the emotions communicated in speech, not merely the words. As Ursa tries to explain to Mama, "If you understood me, Mama, you'd see I was trying to explain it, in blues without words, the explanation somewhere behind the words." Ursa tries to replace the ambiguity of language and the pain of violence with a direct exchange of feeling between two parties. That exchange happens in the multiple levels of communication in the altered, ritualized speech between Mutt and Ursa at the novel's close. Ursa has brought memory with her but it is *her* memory, less oppressive and debilitating, and both characters sing:

> "I don't want a kind of woman that hurt you."
> "Then you don't want me."

Ursa's main task has been to find justice for herself *first,* then the others. Ursa served as nemesis for the women and for Corregidora, as Mutt had been for her. Mutt is also what Albert Murray has called an "antagonistic co-operator"; he helps Ursa break the stranglehold of the past. "Whichever way you look at it," he tells her. "We ain't them." Mutt rejects the ambivalence cultivated by the women as the family's legacy for Ursa. In a brief tale about his own great-grandfather, who tried to contain the anger and bitterness at the sudden loss of his wife by eating contradictory flavors of food, Mutt offers an alternative: "He wouldn't eat nothing but onions and peppermint. Eat the onions so people wouldn't come around him, and then eat the peppermint so they would. I tried it but it didn't do nothing but make me

116

sick" (183–84). Mutt's lesson to Ursa is that justice is not a blues solo of ambivalence or alienation, but a healing communication between reconciled lovers. The voice Ursa gains is the triptych narrative itself, for it returns Ursa to a place of her own and to a quality of evidence and emotion she can sing behind the words.

The action in *Eva's Man* (1976) begins where *Corregidora* left off and envelops us in the despair of one woman's self-inflicted failure to achieve refuge or redemption. The unrelenting violence, emotional silence, and passive disharmony in *Eva's Man* are the undersides of the blues reconciliation and active lovemaking in *Corregidora.* Eva Medina Canada poisons her lover Davis Carter and castrates him with her teeth once he is dead. Important to our brief study here is that Eva never gains control over her voice, her past, her place, or her identity. Instead of wielding language as useful evidence for justice and regeneration as Ursa has done, Eva is defeated by words and brandishes first a pocket knife against Moses Tripp, then arsenic and teeth against Davis. Eva never comes to terms with her past; she chooses to embrace received images of women as *femmes fatales.* Ursa and Eva are further separated by their vastly different ability to experience love.

In view of Jones's concern with opening avenues for reconciliation between the sexes, it is important to see *Eva's Man* and *Corregidora* as companion texts. Primarily through the protagonists' attitudes toward language and their fluency with idioms necessary for personal deliverance, we encounter one woman's fall and another's rise. The clear contrast between them makes Ursa appear as Eva's alter ego and reveals Jones to be a gifted ironist: Eva, surnamed Canada, the promised land and refuge for fugitive slaves, contrasts with Corregidora, Brazilian slave master in one of the larger regions of New World slavery. Yet it is Ursa who frees herself from bondage and Eva who succumbs to it. Eva has chained herself to the debilitating stereotypes of Queen Bee, Medusa, and Eve long before she is locked away in prison for her crime. And Eva is only partly aware of her own responsibility in getting there.

Other contrasts abound. Whereas Ursa is the blues *singer,* who creates musical language and rhythm as evidence of her regeneration, like Hurston's Tea Cake or Walker's Shug Avery, Eva is merely a blues *listener:* "I was sitting in this place eating cabbage and sausage, drinking beer and listening to this woman onstage singing blues" (5). Eva yearns for the reconciliation implicit in a blues exchange that she remembers from her parents arguing "like they were working all that blues out of them or something" (93). One can easily imagine Eva sitting in Happy's Cafe listening to Ursa's hard voice and substituting it in a negative way for her own. Eva wants to gain the kind of control of experience the blues singer seems to possess: "I wanted to make music, hard, deep, with my breath, my tongue inside his mouth. I thought of undoing his trousers, making gestures with my tongue, gestures he'd understand, and then his hands would go into my panties, between my legs and ass" (155).

Ursa uses language more openly and artistically, increasing her awareness of the metaphorical and moral implications of her songs and the persistent echo of her foremothers' pledge. Eva is inarticulate and brutally silent throughout most of the novel, as if she were rebelling against language or had lost her voice completely while filling up on cabbage and sausage and Davis's penis. Davis makes the connection for Eva between himself and food—"You eat food as if you're making love to it" (126)—only to suffer the consequences. Eva refuses to talk to anyone, even when her words would offer evidence in her defense, such as when she knifed Moses Tripp: "I didn't tell anybody . . . I just let the man tell his side" (98). Ursa opens up to Tadpole and Mama and, finally, to Mutt to have the kind of dialogue with history that can break the chain of abuse in the matrilinear descent. Eva shuts herself tight against her own voice and the advice of her mother and Miss Billie. When Eva allows herself to be seduced by Elvira Moody, her cellmate, she passively receives her in the act of cunnilingus ("Tell me when it feels sweet, Eva. Tell me when it feels sweet, honey"), whereas Ursa in the act of fellatio brings Mutt within the orbit of her physical control.

Eva remains imprisoned literally and figuratively by her choice of silence, which simply increases her passivity and allows the words and definitions of others to become hers. Elvira, more like Tadpole and Mutt in *Corregidora* than the rejected lesbian Cat Lawson, tries to get Eva to talk and, by talking, to assume full responsibility for her acts. Eva's silence is more abusive than protective and keeps Eva from performing her own "song" about self and ancestry. Silence also blurs more truth than it reveals, and Eva, unlike Ursa with her foremothers, is unable to gain the larger historical consciousness necessary to end individual alienation. Moreover, Eva's guilty silence, her inability to use language, makes her unable to listen. Eva misses Miss Billie's important advice about the past and being true "to those people who came before you and those people who come after you." Miss Billie, angered and exasperated by her own daughter's disinterest in marriage (in making generations), tries to elicit some response from Eva: "You got to be true to your ancestors and you got to be true to those that come after you. How can you be true to those that come after you if there ain't none coming after you?" (85–86). Eva's deafness to this historical responsibility renders her even more deaf and inarticulate about her own redemption. The prison psychiatrist warns: "You're going to have to open up sometime, woman, to somebody." When Eva opens up, she parts her thighs for Elvira who makes good her threat to make Eva feel something. "You ain't near so hard as you think you are. You think cause you can bite off a man's dick, you can't feel nothing. But you just wait. You gon start feeling, honey. You gon start feeling" (45). When she finally talks, Eva confuses fantasy and reality, unable to tell the difference. Ironically, language fails Eva; it has atrophied from disuse. Eva's sexual coupling with Elvira in prison emphasizes her failure to escape claustrophobic interiors or to utter anything more significant than the chilling "Now" announcing her solo orgasm at the novel's close.

Eva is also defeated by her inability to see Davis for who he is, apart from the other men who have abused her. Rather than acknowledging the part she played in abusing men as Ursa does—which helps her see Mutt more clearly—Eva persists in acting out with Davis the roles of women predators, the characters of Eve, Medusa, and Queen Bee, which are really created by men out of castration anxiety and fears about their repressed femininity. Eva becomes their kind of woman, even to the point of using male language: "I was thinking in the language Alfonso would use" (97). Ursa only sings about the tunnel closing about the train or the bird woman taking the man away and never returning him; Eva accomplishes the deed, but has no language of her own to tell about it. Ursa learns soon enough that Mutt is *not* Corregidora, that reuniting with him can break the stranglehold of the past. Eva confuses Davis with Alfonso, Moses Tripp, and James Hunn. When she finally decides to be active in lovemaking with Davis by making "music hard, deep, with my breath," it is too late. She has already poisoned him. Eva's behavior here is demented and pathetic, a travesty of the successful coupling Ursa achieves with Mutt. Davis, fortunately, is protected in death from feeling the effects of Eva's hunger: "I put my hand on his hand. I kissed his hand, his neck. I put my fingers in the space above his eyes, but didn't close them. . . . I opened his trousers and played with his penis. My mouth, my teeth, my tongue went inside his trousers. I raised blood, slime from cabbage, blood sausage. . . . I spread my legs across his thighs and put his hand on my crotch, stuffed his fingers up in me. I put my whole body over him " (128-29). Eva's active lovemaking with Davis in death is proof of her ultimate failure as a woman trapped in the prison of her emotions, forever singing solo.

Eva fails to deliver herself from the wilderness. She remains "looking like [the] wild woman" she first appeared to be in newspaper photos of her arrest, and she erroneously believes in the surface meaning of the blues song she hears, "Wild Women Don't Get the Blues." Eva misreads the song's irony and Ursa's example. Although Ursa inhabits an interior place of the past in her memory of Corregidora, she succeeds in breaking free. The mountain tunnel releases the train in her song. Ursa travels to another height of self-possession. The geography of the journey for Gayl Jones is both sexual and musical. These two modes of discourse merge in James Baldwin's fiction where similar landscapes, particularly the mountain harboring the tunnel, encompass and transcend desire.

Way up on
the Mountain

CHAPTER FIVE

Rocks gonna cry out:
James Baldwin

Music can get to *be* a song, but it starts with a cry.
— James Baldwin

In 1977 James Baldwin celebrated a partial homecoming after making southern France his refuge since 1948. In an interview with Robert Coles published in the *New York Times,* entitled "James Baldwin Back Home," he discussed his reasons for leaving the United States: "I left America because I had to. . . . I needed to be in a place where I could breathe and not feel someone's hand on my throat" (1). Baldwin's choice of France as a place of retreat was deliberate, for it was there that Richard Wright chose exile a year or so earlier, leaving Baldwin bereft of his newly found mentor and father-figure. Wright was the established writer; Baldwin the neophyte. "For me France was the beginning of a writing life. I wrote *Go Tell It on the Mountain* there. It was there I began the struggle with words" (1).

Although Wright and Baldwin shared France as a haven, they developed contrasting geographical images for places of refuge for their protagonists, drawn partly out of differences in their respective backgrounds and methods. Baldwin was born and bred in Harlem, not in the South; more important, Baldwin grew up within a religious fundamentalism that Wright had grown to despise. Yet both writers, unbeknownst to each other, shared a distrust of religion. Whereas Wright would place his protagonists in underground retreats where they would question and finally reject religion, Baldwin would use religious imagery and structure to create an alternative landscape of his own: the mountain. Whereas Wright would see religion as a sign of the lack of human tenderness and culture in black life (evidenced by his negative characterization of Granny in *Black Boy* and by the wasteland setting of Bigger Thomas's demise in *Native Son*), Baldwin would ferret out the cultural elements in religion, rejecting its dogma that encouraged self-righteousness rather than salvation or fraternal love. Both writers tried to reconcile the contradiction in Protestant fundamentalism that required "being *in* the world but not being *of* the world." Moreover, religion helped Baldwin construct an effective challenge to Wright's naturalistic depiction of black life. By using religious vocabulary, structure, and imagery, Baldwin achieved a figuration of place and person that brought him into community with his protagonists and his reading audience. Baldwin's depiction of John Grimes's religious conversion is a rendering of Baldwin's literary conversion out of the orbit of Wright's domineering influence as his mentor and as a spokesman for blacks. Finally, by manipulating religious expression as a structural device for theme, character development, and narrative tension, Baldwin celebrates the culture transmitted through religious expression. In this way Baldwin gains control of his material, control of his past. Wright's territory of the underground gives way to a broader view of life in the metaphorical space of Baldwin's compelling mountain.

More than a physical representation of place, Baldwin's mountain is a figure for an attitude. His relentless exposé of the guilt and emotional violence meted out in *Go Tell It on the Mountain* (1953) reveals the novel's core to be aesthetic and psychological rather than sociological or theological. Baldwin is more the ironic doubter than devout believer. Leaving the Pentecostal ministry at the age of seventeen, he had exchanged the pulpit for the pen, the sermon for the novel and the essay. In his fiction, he transforms the promise of salvation offered by institutionalized religion into the possibility of conversion and transcendence within a secular spirituality, or humanism, for his characters. His first novel suggests that a discourse on love and shelter may be a key scriptural text to Baldwin's fictional sermon and to our reading of his work. Baldwin's sustained attack on the church as well as his careful unveiling of John's troubled personality occur in two main sections of the novel: "The Seventh Day" and "The Threshing Floor." Both indicate that Baldwin's moral and imaginative geography lies well beyond the social realism or naturalism championed by Wright. Here, Baldwin discovers his unique voice.

Consider the nineteenth-century Negro spiritual from which Baldwin takes his title. The song announces the birth of Christ as well as a speaker's witness of the event. The double movement in the song—a passage into religion and away from it—shows Baldwin's use of religion as a compass to seek refuge, home, and voice:

Go tell it on the mountain,
Over the hills and everywhere;
Go tell it on the mountain,
That Jesus Christ is born.

When I was a seeker,
I sought both night and day,
I asked the Lord to help me,
And he showed me the way.

He made me a watchman
Upon a city wall,
And if I am a Christian
I am the least of all.

Go tell it on the mountain
Over the hills and everywhere;
Go tell it on the mountain
That Jesus Christ is born.

The speaker is not only a watchman upon a city wall, he is also himself a seeker. He announces both the birth of Christ and what the event may mean. The Lord has shown him the way, but he is humble, the least of all Christians. The geographical prominence of the mountain contrasts with the speaker's humility. Only through passage on the low ground of moral vigilance is the speaker able to reach the elevated place required for the important news he carries as an imperative for others. The mountain represents the speaker's spiritual fulfillment and the appropriate stage for its broadcast.

The moral and psychological center of Baldwin's novel is John Grimes, a seeker, a watchman both of the city where he lives and of the lives of his family members. The action takes place on a single day: John's fourteenth birthday, a day filled with his doubt and longing for recognition. *"I looked down the line / And I wondered"* (9) is the novel's apt epigraph for that doubt. The *line* is the narrow way of the elect, the saints, as well as the lineage of his family. John's birthday marks his passage from boyhood to manhood, and his religious initiation marks his passage from being a worldly sinner to becoming an elect saint. But this transformation is almost secondary. John Grimes is converted *out* of religion; he is delivered out of the moral authority of the church and of his preacher stepfather, Gabriel. Using the language, imagery, and structure of religious conversion, *Go Tell*

It on the Mountain tells a radically different story all the better: John's triumph over religion, John's salvation and witness above the *line* measuring the tightly drawn borders of religious fundamentalism. He is a Christian least of all. But as a watchman upon a city wall—indeed, the city itself—he is the seeker who discovers an alternative shelter for his sense of self, sexuality, and love. The mountain represents a pinnacle of self-acceptance for which John yearns. As the day commemorating John's birth ends with his rebirth in the religion that his stepfather has profaned, it also ends with John's first steps away from religion and family. John triumphs over the church and over his stepfather. The image of the mountain that Gabriel uses to justify his spiritual arrogance and self-righteousness is defeated by the threshing floor where John's more complex conversion occurs and where John's completely different journey begins.

Readers are prepared for the spatial dichotomy between the threshing floor and the mountaintop in religious terms by polar configurations in the Harlem urban landscape. Here we find an ironic doubling of two healing institutions; at one end of Lenox Avenue is Harlem Hospital, at the other end the church, the Temple of the Fire Baptized. John remembers the births of his siblings in the former and has premonitions of his rebirth in the latter. These institutions rival each other in granting physical and spiritual salvation with varying degrees of success, and the poles of value shift between them unpredictably. When John's brother Roy is stabbed in a street fight, he needs the hospital more than the church, and as the Grimes family leaves the church at the novel's end, an ambulance careens down the avenue as if to remind them of the mortality of the body if not the soul. This shifting of value between two opposite yet complementary institutions should alert Gabriel to the possibility of an easy fall from his vaunted mountain of moral superiority. Beware the threshing floor. Gabriel takes such delight in mounting high over others in the faith that he is ill-prepared for the spiritual height John ironically achieves on the threshing floor, which diminishes Gabriel's moral authority. John has come out of the wilderness. As Baldwin's prose-sermon tells it: "They wandered in the valley forever; and they smote the rock forever; and the waters sprang, perpetually, in the perpetual desert. They cried unto the Lord forever, and lifted up their eyes forever.... No, the fire could not hurt them and yes, the lion's jaws were stopped; the serpent was not their master, the grave was not their resting place, the earth was not their home ... and, in the fullness of time, the prophet John had come out of the wilderness, crying that the promise was for them" (233). The promise for John Grimes is primarily for himself.

On the morning of the seventh day, John awakens fearful that no one will remember his birthday. His concern about such recognition is not gratuitous, for John is unaware that he is Gabriel's stepson. Gabriel's begrudging notice of John, beyond granting him the family name of Grimes, already charged with meaning, wavers between mild discomfort and blatant hatred. The feeling is mutual. John will end this day winning love and recognition, not from Gabriel but from his spiritual father-brother and Sunday School teacher, Elisha, who serves as John's initiator. John's willingness to experience conversion, to open himself up to "grace," appears to grow out of love and sexual yearning for Elisha. When Elisha poses the question, "Do you want to be saved, Johnny?" (61), John remembers communion Sunday when members of the elect, separated by gender, washed each other's feet and "kissed each other with a holy kiss." Baldwin ends that passage with telling understatement: "John turned again and looked at Elisha" (62).

John is as unsure about religion as he is about his masculinity. His brother Roy taunts him with rough play and by mocking his "shrill little-girl tone" of voice; John in turn affects "as husky a pitch as possible" (23). John's effeminacy is also hinted at by the taunts of children in his neighborhood, particularly the boys' coarse, irreverent voices. John longs "to be one of them playing in the streets, unfrightened, moving with such grace and power, but he knew this could not be" (32). He is troubled by his attraction to Elisha, whose grace and timbre of voice "much deeper and manlier than his own" (12) makes him an object of John's admiration and affection. When John commits the "sin" of masturbation he remembers the boys at school and discovers his unsettling desire: "He had sinned. In spite of the saints, his mother and his father, the warnings he had heard from his earliest beginnings, he had sinned with his hands a sin that was hard to forgive. In the school lavatory, alone, thinking of the boys, older, bigger, braver, who made bets with each other as to whose urine could arch higher, he had watched in himself a transformation of which he would never dare to speak" (18).

In addition to these insecurities, which many boys may feel at the threshold of manhood, John does not know he is Gabriel's stepson. He has no way of deciphering or reckoning with Gabriel's antipathy toward him, other than by acknowledging Gabriel's avowed preference for Roy. Baldwin places John in this situational irony—readers know more than the hero—to magnify the ambiguity of John's position in the family. Baldwin thus makes more urgent John's need to find an alternative home, identity, and morality, as well as a different place from which to ascend to salvation—not climbing the steep side of Gabriel's mountain of hot air, but rising from the more humble threshing floor. John's initial resistance to conversion lies in his refusal to bow down to Gabriel, who imposes his authority with impunity as head of the family and as a church leader (if not as a preacher, then as a "holy handyman" [56]). John comes to the decision, early in the novel, partly out of rebellion against Gabriel, partly out of an awareness of his half-articulated sexuality, that he "would not be like his father, or his father's fathers. He would have another life" (18). John glimpses that other life through Elisha, who ministers to John during his moment of bewildering religious ecstasy when Gabriel is both unwilling and unable to do so. Elisha becomes the cherished agent of initiation who softens John's resistance and eases his fear. John wonders in awe and love "if he would ever be holy as Elisha was holy" (12). Elisha's recognition of John in their playful banter and sensual wrestling, helps to lead John away from Gabriel and to a different place of grace.

Gabriel's failure to recognize John lies in his own sin and guilt, which he has hidden for so long: his denial of his illegitimate son Royal, the death of Royal's mother, Esther, and his constant baiting of Elizabeth to feel as guilty about conceiving John out of her love with Richard as he feels for his adulterous lust with Esther. But these facts, revealed in the powerfully confessional "Prayers of the Saints" section of the novel, are mere exposition to the more symbolic tensions between Gabriel and John that fill the opening chapter, "The Seventh Day," with such ominous meaning.

The name Gabriel prides himself on giving Elizabeth and her nameless son John turns out to be a mixed blessing. Grimes signifies dirt, not only the dirt and grime of human life that can be washed clean through baptism or conversion, but also the moral pollution that clings as tenaciously to the Grimes household as the endless dust John is required to clean: "The room was narrow and dirty; nothing could alter its dimensions, no labor could ever make it clean. Dirt was in the walls and the floorboards, and triumphed beneath the sink where roaches spawned.... Dirt was in every corner, angle, crevice of the monstrous stove.... Dirt was in the baseboard that John scrubbed every Saturday" (21). And there is more dust in the carpet: "John hated sweeping this carpet, for dust rose, clogging his nose and sticking to his sweaty skin, and he felt that should he sweep it forever, the clouds of dust would not diminish, the rug would not be clean. . . . Nor was this the end of John's labor; for, having put away the broom and the dustpan, he took from the small bucket under the sink the dustrag and the furniture oil and a damp cloth, and returned to the living-room to excavate, as it were, from the dust that threatened to bury them, his family's goods and gear" (27–28).

Dirt also pervades the church where John continues his cleaning chores: "In the air of the church hung, perpetually, the odor of dust and sweat; for, like the carpet in his mother's living-room, the dust of this church was invincible" (54). That John's chores should include such work is consistent with Gabriel's view of him and his place in the family, as someone to "clean up" Gabriel's lustful past and become the living proof of his forgiveness from God. Elizabeth, moreover, "was the sign, she and her nameless child, for which he had tarried so many dark years before the Lord. It was as though when he saw them, the Lord had returned to him again that which was lost" (170–71).

To maintain the illusion of his forgiveness and to solidify his righteous domination over Elizabeth, Gabriel constantly reminds her of John's illegitimacy. Using a similar distorted logic, Gabriel had married Deborah, his first wife, both to spite church leaders, who ridiculed her for having been raped by whites, and to set himself high on a mountain of moral righteousness by appearing to redeem Deborah through marriage. (It should be obvious by now that Gabriel is the only grimy person here.) His sins of the past are made more concrete by the presence of a green metal serpent adorning the family mantelpiece. This, John also cleans: "The mantelpiece held, in brave confusion, photographs, greeting cards, flowered mottoes, two silver candlesticks that held no candles, and a green metal serpent, poised to strike" (28).

This serpent, a visual reminder of man's fall from the Garden of Eden and of Gabriel's more contemporary, phallic lust, represents a proud, defiant sexuality: "the green metal serpent, perpetually malevolent, raised its head proudly in the midst of these trophies, biding the time to strike" (29). And strike it does when Gabriel slaps Elizabeth for failing to supervise the wounded Roy. Gabriel brings chaos and violence into the Grimes household. The only person who can control his outbursts and protect Elizabeth is Gabriel's sister, Florence, who holds the key to knowledge about Gabriel's carnal lust and his adulterous past. Florence's handbag contains a letter from his first wife that proves the truth Florence threatens to reveal in the last chapter of the novel: "It'll make Elizabeth to know . . . that she ain't the only sinner . . . in your holy house. And little Johnny, there—he'll know he ain't the only bastard" (245). The one brought low in the threshing floor chapter is Gabriel himself.

Also contributing to Gabriel's fall is his warped view of the mountain. In "Gabriel's Prayer" we see that his vision of the mountain is not a place of retreat or of humble communion with the Lord, but a place of triumph, the parade ground of the elect, a place where he receives the reward of his faith. It is a place not of testing, but of glory. Gabriel's first taste of self-ordained sainthood occurs when he preaches a revival sermon well enough to be seated among the elders in "the upper room of the lodge hall" (120). He is so puffed up with pride that he wishes his mother, who had encouraged him to find religion, could see him, "her Gabriel, mounted so high" (122). Later, his vision is more closely linked with feelings of power and superiority. He sees himself climbing the steep side of a mountain encouraged by a voice to climb higher and higher until he sees a procession (a line?) of the saints. "Touch them not," the voice says. "My seal is on them. . . . So shall thy seed be" (126). Gabriel interprets this as the Lord's voice, without any clear corroboration from Baldwin. Gabriel then marries Deborah and hopes to gain salvation through his progeny, yet when Gabriel fathers Royal from passion and lust for Esther, he never recognizes or takes responsibility for his "seed." Nor does he develop any satisfactory relationship with John, whom he regards as an "interloper among the saints" (129), a stumbling block to his salvation. Gabriel has not loved the human sons who might have carried the "seal" and have redeemed him among the saints, nor has he truly loved the Son of God, despite his sermon against such neglect: "Fathers, think of your sons, how you tremble for them, and try to lead them right, try to feed them so they'll grow up strong; think of your love for *your* son, and how any evil that befalls him cracks up the heart, and think of the pain that *God* has borne, sending down His only begotten Son, to dwell among men on the sinful earth, to be persecuted, to suffer, to bear the cross and *die* —not for His *own* sins, like our natural sons, but for the sins of *all* the world—that we might have the joy bells ringing deep in our hearts tonight!" (117–18).

Gabriel has also failed to heed the welcome motto above the mantelpiece near the green metal serpent or the framed bible passage taken from the Book of John that admonishes love for Christ as God's "only begotten Son," which earns eternal life. Young Roy's cursing of his father and John's silent hatred are proof that Gabriel has failed to heed his own sermon. Gabriel has merely used John and Elizabeth as scapegoats for his hidden sin: "I know you ain't asking me to say I'm sorry I brought Johnny in the world. Is you?" Elizabeth asks. "I ain't going to let you *make* me sorry" (129). Thus, for all Gabriel's hard climb on the steep side of the mountain, he reaches only the cloud bank of his inflated ego and moral cowardice.

John ventures into a different landscape. Not content to be a mere watchman upon a city wall, as in the spiritual, John explores the city. The places of his triumph of self-knowledge, if not, as yet, self-acceptance, occur on the smaller, more human scale of his secular ambitions. His "mountain" is a hill in Central Park that gives him enough positive elation that he is "willing to throw himself headlong into the city that glowed before him" (35). On the hill he decides that the risk of perdition in city life is a more acceptable gamble for him than the cold surety of the narrow way of the saints, the *line* that causes his doubt and wonder. He would have a house and a church and a job like his father. And "he would grow old and black with hunger and toil" (36). This knowledge gives John insight into both ascent to and descent from the moral privilege of saintliness, and he discovers his ability to "climb back up. If it's wrong, I can always climb back up" (37). John's running descent begins his first solo flight: he "began to run down the hill, feeling himself fly as the descent became more rapid" (37). This moment of flight as transcendence of highly charged emotions and on a hilltop or mountain in Baldwin's use of religion will be given more geographical and symbolic figuration in Toni Morrison's use of myth in *Song of Solomon.* John's experience on the hillside brings him a moment of power over himself rather than over others.

Later, during the real test of conversion, the wrenching of his soul on the threshing floor, John finds that the fabled mountain of saintly triumph that Gabriel sought so ruthlessly is more illusory than the positive reward of self-possession awaiting him: "He thought of the mountaintop, where he longed to be, where the sun would cover him like a cloth of gold, would cover his head like a crown of fire, and in his hands he would hold a living rod" (223). These images come from the story of Moses. But where John lay "was no mountain . . . no robe, no crown. And the living rod was uplifted in other hands" (223). The living rod, far from its biblical reference as the serpent and staff of Moses, here signifies sex and lust—the metal serpent on the mantelpiece and the rod of Gabriel's nakedness John had seen.

More startling than the phallic and homoerotic associations is that John's place of salvation and identity lies beyond the valley-mountaintop dichotomy of Christian humility and grace, beyond the male-female coupling gone astray throughout the novel. Herein lies the central problem of John's place in society, and Baldwin's as well: how does one validate a sexual and affectional identity that so profoundly challenges both church and society? Is salvation forever out of reach for us all, forever just above our heads, as a later Baldwin novel suggests, and thus never attainable? John's questioning and doubt seem to parallel Baldwin's own questioning about his place as a writer and critic of institutionalized religion and of relations between blacks and whites. Baldwin hovers at the edge of irresolution in his fiction precisely because the sexual orientation of his protagonists may render their message suspect. Baldwin's male protagonists are usually bisexual or homosexual, and as such they are forever outside the realm of redemption offered either by the church or by society at large. They must come to different terms as best they can with the spatial and spiritual dimensions sanctioned by church and society. Some, like John Grimes, are partly successful. Others end up as suicides, like Rufus Scott in Baldwin's *Another Country*, who leaps in desperation from a bridge. Within this perspective, the need for alternative space, refuge, or shelter looms paramount. John's threshing floor is more than the spatial inverse of Gabriel's mountaintop. It is the place of John's realization of who he is and of the affectional ties that have led him there and now usher him forth into a new life. Elisha becomes John's brother in Christ and a possible lover, although Elisha clearly does not reciprocate the same degree of sexual and emotional interest. John discovers that "to be like [Elisha] is to be loved."

John's fulfillment of character and moral direction does not happen when his conversion ritual ends, but when he and Elisha walk home from church at the novel's close. The space John must claim lies outside the physical boundaries of that institution and outside his home. When John stands at the doorway to his stepfather's house he asserts his new identity and moral power as proof of his deliverance out of confusion and into certainty.

John's conversion is all of a piece, starting from his increasing discontent and hatred of Gabriel, moving to his attraction to Elisha, his replacement of Gabriel with Elisha, and ending with his symbolic "coupling" with Elisha at the novel's close. Elisha's promise to keep the memory of John's conversion seals their bond. John looks Gabriel straight in the eyes for the first time. Gabriel now must pass by him to enter the house. The tension between them is so electric that John seeks another expression of confirmation from Elisha. John must know where this moment will lead him. He tells Elisha, "No matter what happens to me, where I go, what folks say about me, no matter what *anybody* says, you remember—please remember—I was saved. I was *there*" (252). Elisha's "holy kiss" (253) to John seals that memory and the bond between them. When John states, "I'm ready. . . . I'm coming. I'm on my way" (253)—the last lines of the novel—he is a different man indeed. If he goes into Gabriel's house, he goes as a stronger person. The signs we've followed into the novel and into Baldwin's complex moral geography and spiritual search suggest, however, that John Grimes may be lighting out for a completely different territory.

"Havens are high priced," Baldwin argues in *Nobody Knows My Name.* "The price exacted of the haven-dweller is that he contrive to delude himself into believing that he has found a haven" (xii). Perhaps John Grimes's victory is short-lived after all, for one cannot help wondering how he fares in the world beyond storefront churches, tenement stoops, and city parks. Baldwin may also be questioning the validity and usefulness of discoveries made in a retreat or a haven. Should Fred Daniels have remained silent about his knowledge gained underground to save his own life? Is Ellison's protagonist deluding himself into believing he too can resurface? Or is he simply avoiding the act in favor of its verbal shadow? Baldwin hits upon a truth here about the price of remaining in exile; the longer one stays away, the more contrived becomes the delusion (the device?) that the long-sought-for freedom or refuge has been found.

The titles of Baldwin's works after 1953 suggest his ongoing concern with ending the perpetual search for and release from delusion. They also suggest Baldwin's underlying theme that exposes the claustrophobia inherent in the limited space claimed by religious, sexual, or racial exclusivity. *The Amen Corner* depicts the limits Sister Margaret had imposed on herself when she replaced love for her husband with the moral authority of religious salvation. Here she repeats and amplifies Gabriel Grimes's error. Her delusion prevents her from seeing until too late how easy a target she was for jealous church members to usurp her leadership, but in time enough for her to accommodate her son's need for independence and her returned husband's need for comfort in his last days. *Giovanni's Room* examines the emotional cruelty in David's weak acknowledgment of his homosexuality, limited to the charged interior of the bedroom, that fails to free Giovanni from his prison cell. *Another Country* details the racial aspects of Manhattan's landscape where Rufus becomes torn between the integrated life in Greenwich Village and the segregated one in Harlem. The fast life of drugs, music, bisexuality, and interracial coupling are sources for Rufus's creativity and factors of alienation that take him to an urban mountaintop—not the hillside in Central Park, which was the place of John Grimes's epiphany, but the steel structure of the George Washington Bridge. The bridge is an architectural metaphor for Rufus's attempt to merge the vastly different worlds of Harlem and Greenwich Village and of homosexual and heterosexual experiences, both expressed in the racial tension between him (a black northern male) and Leona (a white southern woman). Rufus's suicide after his climb up on the bridge (or up the steel mountain) represents his failure to link the two countries. Love demands his sacrifice. He submits to the air, but he does not fly.

No Name in the Street, a book of essays, echoes Baldwin's preoccupation with his place as writer, black man, and homosexual in American and Afro-American letters. But Baldwin's stance here merely repeats his earlier plea for recognition in the words *Nobody Knows My Name* or in his aborted attempt to become Richard Wright's protégé, if not protagonist, in *Notes of a Native Son.* Baldwin's search for a place to be somebody is his search for a name, a presence as black man, homosexual, bastard son—each a mark of alienation, each a burden Baldwin takes to the streets and to the bridge named for the father of his native land. Baldwin's search for ancestry is his search for a name either in another country or in a room where love and families are made. But such recognition is given grudgingly, if at all. Mostly it remains just above our heads, which is why many readers, I for one, awaited with much anticipation Baldwin's latest novel.

Just Above My Head (1979) represents a dual homecoming for Baldwin. As early as 1977, he had announced in the *New York Times* his intention to return to the United States from France after completing the novel-in-progress. *Just Above My Head* also marked Baldwin's textual homecoming, for as Baldwin implied in the *Times* interview, the new novel actually picks up where *Go Tell It on the Mountain* left off: "I'm going back to France . . . because that's where I can best finish the novel. *Then,* I guess I'll be able to come home. People stop me and say: 'Coming home, Jimmie?' I say yes, soon, but I've got to go back and finish something. Maybe it'll be the end of more than the novel—a long apprenticeship, I sometimes think." And he continued more optimistically and nostalgically, "I remember in those Pentecostal churches when I was young, the tension, the drama, the struggle for a handle on life. I hope I can remember *well*. A person would get up and he'd say, she'd say, to begin with: 'I'm going to step out on the promise.' I guess that's what I'm trying to do" (24).

Such a step of homecoming and promise weighs heavily on author and readers alike. It is a major gamble technically and thematically. John Grimes's departure and alienation from his family is "corrected" and "revised" in *Just Above My Head* when Hall Montana attempts to reconcile himself to race, family, and heterosexuality by narrating his homosexual brother's life. These "havens" have their price, and Hall's sentimentality and presumptuousness (his arrogant rendition of Arthur's emotions and sexuality about which he could know nothing) contribute to the novel's undoing. Baldwin's quest for transcendence (from sexual and racial labels) and his climb up the steep side of the mountain fail to address the central paradox in most of his fiction: the inability to reconcile the emotional (affectional) needs of a homosexual artist who expresses himself in a verbal art based in the religion that ultimately condemns him. Hall's narration of the life of gospel singer Arthur Montana (Spanish for "mountain") is merely one brother's manipulation of another to come to terms with his conventional responsibilities to family and to self. For Baldwin to allow this to happen indicates that his homecoming may not be as complete or as honestly fulfilling as he would have us think. Perhaps homecoming and home are havens that produce only more elaborately contrived delusions about their gifts of shelter and refuge.

In spite of Baldwin's lengthy introduction of his narrator as a regular guy, readers never get beyond him and to Arthur, the subject of the novel. And it is too far into the text before Hall finally admits what readers had suspected all along: "It was not meant to be my story, though it is far more my story than I would have thought, or might have wished" (529). The novel remains unfortunately beyond the reach of its narrator, but it is filled with a complexity of spatial imagery that only confirms Baldwin's principal theme to be reconciliation—largely in contrast to the kind of alienation he so vividly depicted in *Go Tell It on the Mountain.* The realization Hall comes to about family and inheritance redirects us to the novel's message of place, person, and the meaning of performance: "An inheritance is a given: in struggling with this given, one discovers oneself in it—and one could not have been found in any other place!—and, with this discovery, and not before, the possibility of freedom begins" (483).

Baldwin's characterization of Arthur Montana arises out of Baldwin's previous attempt to reconstruct an image of the Afro-American family where the dynamics of love and mutual support help the family persevere, survive. This is the strikingly noble yet overly sentimental theme of *If Beale Street Could Talk,* a transitional novel in Baldwin's canon because it moves us beyond the alienation of race (as in *Another Country*), sexuality (*Giovanni's Room*), or religion (*The Amen Corner*). Baldwin tries to capture the essence of an Afro-American spiritualism not rooted in institutional religion but just above it, in that curiously amorphous realm of humanism (secular spirituality). The key to this concept in Baldwin's most recent novel is the narrator-turned-protagonist Hall, whose increasingly apparent struggle to love and accept Arthur is the submerged drama in *Just Above My Head.*

Significantly, Arthur Montana is not the preacher everyone once hoped John Grimes would become; he is a gospel singer, a performing artist who occupies an ambiguous and intermediary position between preacher and congregation. Arthur's homosexuality turns that ambiguity into a paradox, the dimensions of which escape Hall. But readers are brought back to Baldwin's central dilemma: how to reconcile an aberrant sexuality with a religion that condemns it as sin. Yet most artists are living paradoxes: products of, critics to, and supporters of a cultural community. An artist belongs to a community, a language, a historical experience. The artist's freedom comes in the discovery of that inheritance. No less is true of the gospel singer who both professes religion through his art form and refashions art through his religion. He is at once an insider and outsider, a believer, true, but a performer who must arouse belief and commitment in others by his living witness to sin and salvation. As Hall says of Arthur: "His love was his confession, his testimony was his song" (261). Or as Arthur himself explains, "When you sing . . . you can't sing *outside* the song. You've got to *be* the song you sing. You've got to make a confession" (55). Who can best testify to spiritual elevation than one who is downtrodden, burdened by "sin" or "transgressions" that make passage into salvation all the more dramatic, urgent, and instructive for others? Is this why Arthur's life becomes so useful to Hall, who needs an anchor, an example, to embrace the "inheritance" of his past, to meet the needs of his present family?

Such an ironic reversal of narrator-to-protagonist is not new in Baldwin's fiction. A similar schema emerges from his short story "Sonny's Blues." A brilliant story ostensibly about a fledgling young jazz musician, Sonny, it develops into a revealing emotional portrait, if not story, about the narrator, Sonny's older brother. This unnamed figure has difficulty expressing grief at the death of his daughter and fulfilling a promise made to his dying mother to look after the wayward Sonny, whom he does not understand. He has taken refuge behind a bland lower middle-class life in the same confining space his parents occupied—a housing project in Harlem—and in his conventional career as a junior high school algebra teacher. The narrator's exasperated tone in describing Sonny's life exposes his unarticulated desire to break out of stifling routine, which he does when he finally *listens* to Sonny's music and offers a curiously symbolic drink of Scotch and milk as an offer of reconciliation following Sonny's performance of a solo. The ambivalent mixture of Scotch and milk represents the efforts at nurture and release into adult independence that the narrator gives Sonny at the story's end.

Hall Montana, another troubled older brother, uses his "biography" of Arthur as a way to articulate his "autobiography." Yet Hall occasionally sidesteps the more painful and threatening aspects of Arthur's life, although Arthur has always been honest with him. Hall reveals his difficulty in accepting his brother and loving him despite his countless words to the contrary. When his son, Tony, comments after Arthur's death: "They say—he was a faggot." Hall replies haltingly: "Arthur slept with a lot of people—mostly men, but not always. He was young, Tony. Before your mother, I slept with a lot of women . . . mostly women, but—in the army—I was young, too—not always. You want the truth; I'm trying to tell you the truth. . . . Whatever the fuck your uncle was, and he was a whole lot of things, he was nobody's faggot" (30). As Hall unfolds Arthur's life, readers cannot escape Arthur's calm assertion that baffles Hall: "But I *am* a sissy" (22). Although the details of Hall's answer to Tony are revealing, Hall fails to satisfy Tony's honest question. The novel is Hall's attempt to relieve his evasiveness and to examine if not the lower "frequencies" of Arthur's death ("in a men's room in the basement of a London pub" [5]), then the heights reached in Arthur's career and personality that are, for the most part, beyond Hall's reach. Note that Hall's description of heterosexual lovemaking with his wife Ruth becomes the contrived haven Baldwin has continually warned us about: "Kneeling, I kiss her legs, her thighs, my lips, my tongue, move upward to her sex, her belly button, her breasts, her neck, her lips, and I hold her in my arms, like some immense, unwieldy treasure. I, at least, thank God that I come out the wilderness. My soul shouts hallelujah, and I do thank God" (17). Hall's heterosexuality seems a poorly constructed shelter in his retreat from the moral "wilderness" of Arthur's life and sexuality. No haven, not even the narration of a novel, seems without its contrivance, its device.

The church is another key haven, both in Baldwin's life (and he details this refuge in *The Fire Next Time*) and in his fiction. His critique of the church in *Go Tell It on the Mountain* reappears in *Just Above My Head* as a behind-the-scenes look at the religious posturing and false elevation of the child evangelist, Julia. 'Her rise to influence is engineered by her hustler father, who becomes her pimp, refusing, later, to let her abandon the lucrative ministry. The artificiality of her righteousness is emphasized by the contraption that holds her up and by her father who literally pulls the strings: "This was a special, collapsible platform, constructed by her father. . . . The hidden platform looked like a wooden box, with a rope handle. When her father opened it, with his boyish flourish, the box became a platform with one short step, and the rope handle became a handrail, sometimes painted gold. This contraption, and her father, traveled with Julia everywhere: and made Julia's appearance in the pulpit seem mystical, as though she were being lifted up" (65). When Julia eventually abandons this religion—once her father completes his role as "pimp" by raping Julia and leading her into prostitution ("I was looking at ceilings" [380])—Arthur begins his professional ministry of song. Hall is a troubled witness to both worlds and to the acts of ascent and descent accompanying them.

Hall's role as reluctant witness is revealed in the following admission: "Arthur lived in a world I only glimpsed, sometimes, through him: I didn't really pay my dues in that world, not the way he did" (13). Hall's grand confession, his quest for reconciliation (with Arthur, with Julia, and with his parents by remembering their lives) is ultimately unsuccessful. He has refused to take a leap of faith in love for Arthur that would help him to relate Arthur's life more completely—which no one but Arthur can do, really. A narrator can hope only for a fuller understanding of his own life. Whether Hall achieves this is questionable. He relinquishes the narrative at a key point—and a jarring one for readers—to Jimmy, Arthur's lover of fourteen years and Julia's younger brother for whom she, like Hall, has presumably made sacrifices. It is left to Jimmy to narrate the more intimate details of Arthur's last years on the road in the United States and touring throughout Europe.

Hall's objective is to return Arthur within the orbit of family, and this becomes the way Hall can finally mourn Arthur's passing. To paraphrase one of the gospel songs in the novel, Arthur becomes the stone (the rock that cries out?) that Daniel (Hall) saw hewed out the mountain, which is Baldwin's geographical metaphor for the history, love, and identity we must all face. Hall's concern now is for his children, Tony and Odessa. For himself, he confesses, "I am not reconciled" (530), yet he holds out a last possibility of escape through a weak rationalization:

> Not one of us saw our futures coming: we lived ourselves into our present, unimaginable states, until, abruptly, without ever having achieved a future, we were trying to decipher our past. Which is all right, too, I guess, on condition that one does not consider the past a matter for tears, recriminations, regrets. I am what I am, and what I have become. I wouldn't do it over if I could, and, if I could, if I had to do it over, I wouldn't know how. The very idea causes the spirit within me to grow faint with fatigue. No Thank you: I do not forget that fire burns, that water overwhelms, rolls, and drags you under, that madness awaits in the valley, the mirror, and on the mountaintop. I have no regrets. . . . I will carry on from here, thank you. My hand is on the Gospel plow, and I wouldn't take nothing for my journey now. (530–31)

Hall's speech is littered with phrases from the gospel songs Arthur sang so beautifully. Perhaps Hall does become reconciled to Arthur and to his own past in the only way left him, by telling his own story through a language drawn from Arthur's profession and partly from his recognition of the small part of his brother's life in which he can participate. *"Hall Montana Presents"* (the publicity bulletins announcing Arthur's concerts when Hall was his manager) not Arthur, but Hall himself, imbued with a language of basic truth (the literal meaning of gospel: good news, a kind of truth-telling). Hall's truthful witness lies not in the details of Arthur's life, but in what he learns from Arthur's emotional honesty, which helps him, finally, to communicate more openly with Tony and Odessa and Ruth and Julia in their later lives, and with us as readers. What Hall offers to Arthur is not the ambivalence of Scotch and milk, but another cup of trembling, a narrative about himself as filtered through Arthur's life or through Hall's climb to the mountaintop of self-acceptance from the underground tremors of Arthur's basement death. Hall's language, filled more eloquently with the life he both tells and refuses to tell, becomes his bridge in the air, which is one way of crossing the "conundrum of space" and reuniting with a former lover, brother, or self. Whereas the steel bridge Rufus climbed signaled his inability to cross, the verbal bridge Hall constructs helps him over the chasm of generations. Both characters use Baldwin's figure of a mountaintop as a "conundrum of space" to be solved. In this manner, Baldwin sets the stage for Toni Morrison's more physical, concrete depiction of what it takes to climb the mountain and to conquer it through flight.

CHAPTER SIX

Like an eagle in the air: Toni Morrison

In recent interviews Toni Morrison has talked about her midwestern, Ohio background and the possibilities it presents for new settings in Afro-American fiction. "It's an interesting state from the point of view of black people because it is right there by the Ohio River, in the south, and at its northern tip is Canada. And there were these fantastic abolitionists there, and also the Ku Klux Klan lived there. . . . So I loved writing about that because it was so wide open" (*Chant,* 215). On another occasion she remarked, "Ohio offers an escape from stereotyped black settings. It is neither plantation nor ghetto" (Tate, 119). From a home that is neither typically North nor South, Morrison, like Ellison, who comes from Oklahoma, freely explores new physical and metaphorical landscapes in her fiction. She envisions space with fewer historically or politically fixed boundaries and endows her characters with considerable mobility. Her play of language upon and from within the land creates areas of symbolic activity for both author and protagonists: house and yard become scenes of psychological dislocation in *The Bluest Eye* (1970); land gradations and moral codes have inverted meaning in *Sula* (1973); mountain, farm, and island emerge as stages for enacting dramas of self-creation, racial visibility, and cultural performance in *Song of Solomon* (1977) and in *Tar Baby* (1981). Starting with her birthplace in Lorain, Ohio, and subsequent transformations of that place into several charged fields in fiction, Toni Morrison has imagined a complex and multitextured world.

The symbolic geography in Morrison's fiction emerges from the precise physical details that give her black neighborhoods so much startling character and presence. Medallion, Ohio, or Shalimar, Virginia, fixes firmly in the imagination and shapes either terrestrial or celestial images through which

Morrison initiates a dialogue with earlier texts discussed in this study, most notably with Ralph Ellison's *Invisible Man.* In the three novels that have earned Morrison an indisputable prominence in contemporary American letters, the author enlarges and completes many previous attempts to show the importance of both place and person in the development of Afro-American culture. From the songs her characters sing to transform otherwise dreary households into spiritual havens, and from the journeys they undertake through history and myth as in the early slave narratives (as the author revealed, "You know, I go sometimes and, just for sustenance, I read those slave narratives—there are sometimes three or four sentences or half a page, each one of which could be developed in an art form, marvelous" [*Chant,* 229]) comes the achievement of form and art in Morrison's fiction.

Attentive to the physical and cultural geography of the small black towns that have shaped her and her characters, Morrison constructs familiar yet new dialectical oppositions between enclosed and open spaces, between the fluid horizontality of neighborhoods (shifting, migrating populations, a profusion of character types and changing morals) and the fixed verticality, hence presumed stability, of the house. Morrison calls for an end to Ellisonian inertia and a delight in the free fall. These oppositions produce various exciting results that propel characters and readers toward the principal movement in Morrison's fiction: the leap from land into sky. Pecola Breedlove, for one, ventures to the "cave" of Elihue's mind (the cerebral force, readers will recall, that pushed Ellison's protagonist to consider ending his underground hibernation, "Because, damn it, there's the mind, the *mind.* It wouldn't let me rest" [433]) and its reservoir of conjure and magic. Pecola comes away with the cherished blue eyes that she alone can see (a blindness that completes the invisibility she had suffered from others). She wears a vision of the sky but never gains its reward of flight (is the name Pecola a variant of peacock?). For Pecola's aesthetic choice sinks her evermore into the mire of self-hatred that had initially created her desire. Sula, on the other hand, longs for flight and song but gets no farther than the upper rooms of Eva's house of death. The house opposes the space of Ellison's cellar, but it is filled with the same inertia (the stunted growth of the eternally juvenile Deweys is one example). The one character who eventually learns to resist the gravitational pull of social conformity and to grasp what his newly stretched imagination can reach is Milkman Dead. He earns the authority to sing his real name, for he not only has discovered the long-sought-for-ancestor Solomon, he becomes him when he tries the air.

That test of the air—the risk, the ultimate surrender to it, and the strengthening *ride*—culminates Morrison's metaphorical triumph over conventional terrestrial frontiers or boundaries to identity, moving up into the celestial infinity of its achievement. Milkman's journey from No Mercy Hospital to the cave in Danville, Pennsylvania, and from a wilderness hunt to a mountaintop discovery in Shalimar, Virginia, offers a more satisfying solution to black homelessness than the reflective yet artificial hibernation Ellison had proposed.

The Bluest Eye. "When the land kills of its own volition"

Claudia MacTeer, the occasional and maturing narrator in Morrison's first novel, discovers one of the earth's peculiar traits that may mitigate the guilt she feels for the failure of her marigold seeds to grow: *"For years I thought my sister was right: it was my fault. I had planted* [our seeds] *too far down in the earth. It never occurred to either of us that the earth itself might have been unyielding"* (3). This revelation brings only partial relief. It offers one explanation of the novel's theme: the loss of innocence. The underlying question concerns the earth's role in bringing on misfortune, in creating a climate for Pecola's suffering and insanity as well as confusing the parameters of moral responsibility. The actual telling of the story, the sharing of narration among several voices, including Pauline's interior monologues, leads Claudia to confess too late the community's and her own complicity in acquiescing to hostility by taking life's misery too much for granted. "We acquiesce and say the victim had no right to live. We are wrong, of course, but it doesn't matter. It's too late" (164). The victim here is not only Pecola's premature and dead baby, sired by Pecola's own father, but also Pecola herself. The loss of Claudia's and Frieda's innocence, as they witness and report Pecola's decline, makes them victims as well.

The Bluest Eye is Morrison's study of a community out of touch with the land and the history that might have saved them. The displacement of blacks had begun long before Claudia's retrospective narration about the failed marigolds. The distance between their lives and the ideal American home or family, depicted in the passage from the grade-school reader that opens the novel, is also measured by the increasingly distorted passage, parts of which later introduce the subject of each subsequent chapter. This technique reveals the pervasive trauma of dislocation suffered by Pecola, Claudia, Soaphead Church, and the entire community.

The grade-school text is designed primarily to teach language skills by describing supposedly familiar situations lodged in social myths of education and upward mobility. The environment evoked by Mother, Father, Dick, and Jane in their neat little house and yard with the requisite cat and dog juxtaposes starkly against the lives of the pupils who are learning to read. They do learn their position outside the text as readers, but, more important, their place outside the "home" and "neighborhood" depicted here. Pecola's distance from the text and from society increases greatly when her most intimate spaces—the home and parts of the body—are violated when she is raped by her father. Pecola's deteriorating emotional balance and the trouble witnessed by Frieda and Claudia that forces their early maturation appear first in a gradual compression of print in the passage until the words jumble together. The distortion represents the girls' actual education. The syntactical and typographical disorder reveals the increasing violation of physical, social, and personal space. The position of the words and set of type on the page as well as that of reader to the text have been altered not only by the difference between ideal and actual settings, but also by those forces in society that constantly displace individuals by offering negative refuge. Morrison returns us once again to the prototypical nameless, homeless, landless situation of black Americans in literature and in society. The myth of recovery and replacement and the false hope Pecola constructs—having blue eyes—are more damaging.

The concern for place and home hinted at by the grade-school text is developed further in Claudia's description of her neighborhood and the difference between her house and Pecola's storefront residence. Their respective homes indicate more than a difference in social class; they set the stage for Morrison's view of the ambivalent attraction and repulsion of the middle class for lower-class vitality. In Morrison's later novels, the prissy Nel is drawn to Sula's "woolly house" (29) and bourgeois Milkman Dead finds vibrant life in the disorder at Pilate's ramshackle cabin. Morrison is less concerned with class conflict, however, than with the spontaneous affirmation of cultural and spiritual well-being that exists outside the borders of middle-class respectability.

"Our house is old, cold, and green" (5), says Claudia, bringing to mind a variation of the "green and white" house in the grade-school text. Claudia's assessment of place and house introduces her perception of black homelessness and wilderness that motivates an almost desperate urge to own property and secure refuge. Cholly Breedlove violates the primacy of the home in an affront to middle-class aspirations by burning his storefront dwelling and putting his family out. He incurs Claudia's wrath and exposes her insecurity as well as her fear of homelessness and the uncertain outdoors (a wilderness of sorts): "If you are put out, you go somewhere else, if you are outdoors, there is no place to go" (11). Outdoors becomes the real terror of the middle class, a grim reminder of their political and economic vulnerability. To relieve this insecurity, people buy property with a vengeance. Cholly Breedlove, however, a "renting black" (12), exists apart from this class concern. His violent behavior turns his son Sammy into a perennial runaway and his daughter Pecola into a welfare "case" (11), which is how she enters the MacTeer family temporarily and begins a precarious friendship with Frieda and Claudia. Breedlove, in his disdain for property (burning his residence) and family (putting them out*doors*) is seen as part of the moral as well as physical wilderness: "having put his family outdoors [he] had catapulted himself beyond the reaches of human consideration. He had joined the animals, was, indeed, an old dog, a snake, a ratty nigger" (12). He lands in jail. Until her family is reunited, Pecola has more than a taste of the comfortable life: she drinks three quarts of milk a day from a Shirley Temple glass.

The Breedloves' storefront residence is a "box of peeling gray" (25) on the top floor of which live several prostitutes: China, Poland, and the Maginot Line (Miss Marie), named for landscapes they would neither visit nor represent. The whores become a surrogate family to Pecola, for they are comfortable in their profession, their self-chosen place. They offer Pecola a social education her more-displaced mother refuses to give. Pauline, who "never felt at home anywhere, or that she belonged anyplace" (86), finds a world where her sense of order, arrangement, and privacy can have full reign, working, ironically, as a maid for the white Fisher family. They not only allow Pauline this private, self-defined space, but also give her a nickname so place-specific that it signifies both the "illusion" of privacy and its invasion each time she is called Polly. More devastating is Pauline's proprietary selfishness; she refuses to share the kitchen with her own children: "Pauline kept this order, this beauty, for herself, a private world, and never introduced it into her storefront, or to her children" (100). Given such maternal neglect, it is small wonder that Pecola would also seek an illusion of beauty in wanting blue eyes.

Morrison's further explorations into the relation between person and place, between identity (visible or invisible) and land center in the lives of

Pecola and Cholly and inform all of her fiction. Invisibility is foisted upon Pecola not only because she is black and female, but also because she is ugly. She suffers "the total absence of human recognition—the glazed separateness" (36), alienating her from others. Cholly, when young, mired himself in ugly behavior and self-hatred when he started to see himself as negatively as whites viewed him. On the night following his Great-Aunt Jimmy's funeral, Cholly was caught in the act of making love in the woods by white hunters. The flashlight they shone on his nakedness also illuminated their view of him: "Get on wid it, nigger. . . . An' make it good" (116). Turning his rage inward and onto Darlene instead of at the whites, Cholly experiences the self-hatred he will later inspire in Pauline and Pecola. Furthermore, the physical ugliness that makes Cholly and Pecola so visible that they are invisible also makes them, in Claudia's view, willful prisoners of their shabby storefront: "They lived there because they were poor and black, and they stayed there because they believed they were ugly" (28).

What might have redeemed Cholly in his own eyes and have prevented the internalization of ugliness was his search for his estranged father. Cholly's journey when young had led him not to the "green and white" (1) house of social myth, nor to the "old, cold, and green" (5) house of the black middle class, but to the folded greenbacks poking from the fists of city gamblers. Among them he finds his father, who is more interested in scoring a hit than recognizing his son. Crushed by this rejection, Cholly loses control of himself (indeed, his very bowels) and retreats into the woods. There by the Ocmulgee River, he washes himself and his clothes in a kind of purification ritual, which is complete only when pent-up tears of grief and loneliness finally cascade down his face. Cholly had been prepared to show his grief (a form of recognition itself) by nesting in the woods ("the dark, the warmth, the quiet, enclosed Cholly like the skin and flesh of an elderberry protecting its own seed" [124]), undressing, and feeling about on his hands and knees for the cleansing edge of water. When he cries, he becomes the "new young boy" (125) who will be received back in town by three women offering him lemonade and his manhood through sex. But the freedom Cholly experiences so briefly needs connections to be fully meaningful, even to Cholly, and he longs for a song to sing to activate his new identity. Lacking the music, his transformation and self-confidence are all too brief:

> The pieces of Cholly's life could become coherent only in the head of a
> musician. Only those who talk their talk through the gold of curved

metal, or in the touch of black-and-white rectangles and taut skins and strings echoing from wooden corridors, could give true form to his life. Only they would know how to connect the heart of a red watermelon to the asafetida bag to the muscadine to the flashlight on his behind to the fists of money to the lemonade in a Mason jar to a man called Blue and come up with what all of that meant in joy, in pain, in anger, in love, and give it its final and pervading ache of freedom. Only a musician would sense, know, without even knowing that he knew, that Cholly was free. (125)

Without music, Cholly's freedom has no voice, no meaningful or cohering performance to tie together the loose tangling strands of his life thus far. His failure to act upon or act with the identity he has discovered renders his freedom tenuous, his virility inadequate. Cholly's one effort to make connections to the past and present through love results in his rape of Pecola. Cholly had perceived Pecola's unconscious and innocent scratching of her leg with the opposite foot as a reminder of the moment he had fallen in love with Pauline, who was leaning against a road fence—like Hurston's Janie—"scratching herself with a broken foot" (126). Cholly's warped confusion of time and place becomes his odd performance. His one effort to heal displacement ends up sending Pecola and Pauline more out*doors* than before, right to "the edge of town."

Pecola's rape neither begins nor completes her emotional disintegration. That deed is left to Soaphead Church, another figure alienated from the land ("Dear God: . . . Once upon a time I lived greenly and youngish on one of your islands" [140]), who had accepted the nickname in exchange for his false conjure and magic. He grants Pecola's wish for blue eyes. His appearance and act in the novel as a *deus ex machina* borrowed from drama are more diabolical than Cholly's deed, which at least offered Pecola a kind of love and recognition, however perverted. Soaphead offers insanity. Both men keep Pecola grounded—if not pinned bodily—to the kitchen floor until she loses consciousness or becomes mired in schizophrenia and delusion. Both family and community, loved ones and landscape, have banished Pecola. A devastating inertia prevents her from achieving the flight she thought would come with the blue eyes. Pecola wears a vision of the sky (like Cholly's search for transcendent, cohering music) but fails to achieve its reward of flight: "The damage done was total. She spent her days, her tendril sap-green days, walking up and down, up and down, her head jerking to the beat of a drummer so distant only she could hear. Elbows bent, hands

147

on shoulders, she flailed her arms like a bird in an eternal, grotesquely futile effort to fly. Beating the air, a winged but grounded bird, intent on the blue void it could not reach—could not even see—but which filled the valleys of the mind" (162).

As Pecola scavenges through garbage, her birdlike gestures diminish "to a mere picking and plucking her way between the tire rims and the sunflowers, between Coke bottles and milkweed, among all the waste and beauty of the world" (162), and Claudia realizes the extent to which Pecola had absorbed the waste she and others had dumped on her. In return Pecola simply gave the only beauty she had: her innocence. Claudia, now mature, realizes that the failure of marigold seeds to grow that year was not only the fault of "the earth, the land, of our town" (164), but hers as well. Having acquiesced to the easy victimization of Pecola, Claudia had failed to acknowledge the earth's own will to kill and the readiness of humans to accomplish the deed.

Sula. "It's the bottom of heaven—best land there is"

A more complex figuration of land and identity emerges in *Sula.* Beyond the psychological boundaries that imprison Pecola and allow the MacTeer sisters to bear witness to the loss of sexual and mental place, *Sula* tells the story of two women who renegotiate the pressures of place and person through their long friendship, which is not without moments of rupture and discord. The growing bond between Nel Wright and Sula Mae Peace as well as their complementary personalities are first revealed to us by the contrasting features of the land.

Two key terrestrial images frame the novel: the hillside signifying the creation of the black community of Medallion, Ohio, known as the Bottom (through the chicanery of a white planter unwilling to fulfill his promise of valley land to an industrious and newly emancipated slave), and a tunnel under construction at New River Road that collapses upon participants in Shadrack's last march to commemorate National Suicide Day. At first glance, the hillside and the tunnel appear dichotomous. The hillside, or the Bottom, is named ironically, and it is viewed through a passing of time: "there was once a neighborhood." The phrase introduces a narrative about an entire community, but also prophesies its destruction, the hell of mutability alluded to by Nel: "Hell ain't things lasting forever. Hell is change" (108).

One reading of these two regions suggests they have male and female characteristics: the phallic hillside and the vaginal tunnel, particularly when one recalls that the Bottom was established as a black community through a barter between two men. But Morrison gives the two regions feminine traits and infuses them with a preponderance of female properties, in the dual sense. One then suspects a different personification at work. Irene's Palace of Cosmetology, Reba's Grill, the dance of a "dark woman in a flowered dress doing a bit of cakewalk, a bit of black bottom, a bit of 'messing around' to the lively notes of a mouth organ" (4), all depict a procreative, female environment. The hillside is nurturing; it is a veritable breast of the earth. Within a feminine figuration (accompanying the narrative of a nurturing friendship between Nel and Sula) the hillside complements rather than contrasts with the womblike tunnel, which upon "breaking water" becomes a haunting, unsuspecting grave when several Bottom luminaries drown. This "abortion" of life occurs right at the time Medallion is undergoing a kind of rebirth through urban renewal. Whites and blacks are changing geographical spaces: the former moving to the cooler hills, the latter descending to the crowded valley floor. This change and death reverse the notion of economic upward mobility for Medallion blacks, who have only a promise of work on New River Road, and foreshadow the further decline, or bottoming *out,* of the community. The nurture-destruction tension in Morrison's figuration of the land this early in the novel more than prepares us for the complementary relationship, shifting moral dualism, and irony between Sula Mae Peace, who makes and unmakes peace in the community, and Nel Wright, who is never fully as right or as morally stalwart as she would like to appear.

The double figuration of the land as a framing device also foreshadows the novel's curiously double closure. One ending, effected by Shadrack's haunting, successful celebration of death, culminates his search for a "place for fear" as a way of "controlling it" (14) and brings his social marginality to a shocking conclusion. A second ending, however, forces the reader to revise this reading of the novel. Nel's visit to the elderly Eva, now in a nursing home, picks up the unfinished business between Nel and Sula (here represented by Eva) with shattering results: Nel is forced to acknowledge the guilt she shares with Sula for the accidental drowning of Chicken Little, who had slipped from Sula's swinging hands and had entered the "closed place of the water" (61). The scene also foreshadows the tunnel's sudden collapse. Nel must also acknowledge the grief for Sula she had tried to suppress, only to discover in her solitary walk home that grief like guilt has no prescribed boundaries; it demands open public expression. When she realizes the extent of her accountability to Sula's friendship—"We was girls together"—Nel lets loose the emotion she had artificially held in check all these years: the cry without "bottom" or "top," but "circles and circles of sorrow" (174). The ever-spiraling geometry of Nel's grief returns readers to the scene of Chicken Little's death and forces us to rethink and replace the event. Sula's "evil" now appears innocuous and Nel's guilt more calculating and malevolent. We must also reconsider Nel's [W] rightness, for her cry admits a moral responsibility for wrongdoing that was not Sula's alone. Riding the spiral of Nel's grief back through the novel, we encounter other geometrical and geographical images that clearly establish the theme of moral dualism and double meaning in society and in nature. *Sula* then becomes as much a novel about the shifting patterns of accountability in Sula and Nel's friendship as it concerns a community's acceptance of moral relativism.

The boomerang effect of the shifting moral and physical geography of Medallion, Ohio, can be seen, for example, in the medallion Sula wears, the birthmark above her eye, the meaning of which changes according to who reads it. Morrison's novel is as much about interpretation as it is about art. How members of the community *read* Sula tells us a great deal about their relation to the land, to themselves, and to the meaning they create. The first indication of this theme is the novel's epigraph, taken from *The Rose Tattoo,* which implicates an entire community, a "they," in the speaker's nonconformist assertion of self: *"Nobody knew my rose of the world but me. . . . I had too much glory. They don't want glory like that in nobody's heart."* No one really knows Sula or why she sets about—as she tells Eva—to "make herself." But nearly everyone has an opinion about Sula's medallion: a sign they believe of her "evil," her *"too much glory"* in flaunting her disregard of social conventions. At first Sula's birthmark is described as a "stemmed rose" (52); as she matures, it becomes a "stem and rose" (74), suggesting the duality in nature as well as Sula's developing thorny yet attractive personality. With age, the mark becomes "the scary black thing over her eye" (97-98). When Jude begins to see the mark as a "copperhead" (103) and a "rattlesnake" (104), he is seduced by Sula. And as Sula becomes the evil the community fears yet abides, her mark indicates either "Hannah's ashes" (114) or, as Shadrack sees it, "a tadpole" (156). No one, not even Nel, knows Sula's heart. Indeed, Sula's closest kin, in terms of the community's social and moral landscape, is none other than Shadrack, whose madness makes him at once both an outsider and insider: "Once the people understood the boundaries and nature of his madness, they could fit him, so to speak, into the scheme of things" (15). His shack in the woods or wilderness, halfway between the order of the town and the disorder of the lake where Chicken Little drowned, becomes Sula's refuge, a more useful shelter after the accident than Nel's calculated silence. When Shadrack answers "always" (62) to the distraught Sula's unvoiced question, he seals the doubling of their characters in one word of recognition.

The shifting geometry of Sula's birthmark also shapes her actions throughout the novel and identifies the forces directing her. Readers will recall that we know nothing of Sula's life away from Medallion—her time spent in college, in New York, and in other parts of the country—because Sula's real character, however enigmatic, comes from this community, this Medallion. It is her home and, as suggested above, her landmark. When Sula returns home after an absence of ten years, she fully claims the territory as hers by dispossessing Eva of the house. Sula then occupies Eva's third floor bedroom. Her hibernation behind the boarded window seals her fate in the family and in the community. Sula's appropriation of height in the upper room does not, however, bring the desired refuge or elevation. Nor does it become the place of performance where the creation of character, the "making of oneself" can take place. Although she repossesses a space, Sula, like Cholly Breedlove, fails to find therein a voice for her identity. The self she finds in the house where she was born is still incomplete, as fragile and infantile as her uncle Plum. When Eva descended the stairs on her one leg—the only time she actually went down those stairs—she found Plum in a stupor of drug addiction, trying to return to her womb. Childlike, he clearly needed a new identity, a new birth, but one that Eva could neither provide nor accommodate. She set fire to him. Plum's vision before he burned to death may offer a clue to Sula's fate: "He opened his eyes and saw what he imagined was the great wing of an eagle pouring a wet lightness over him. Some kind of baptism, some kind of blessing, he thought" (47). Plum succumbs to the "bright hole of sleep" (47) without achieving flight on the eagle's wing. Sula, who had returned to Medallion during a plague of robins, also yearns for flight as the fulfillment of the self-creation she thought she had achieved. In the upper room, now the setting for her ardent lovemaking with Ajax, Sula discovers her human frailty (sexual possessiveness and emotional vulnerability). It is also the place where she dies.

151

Flight appears in Morrison's oeuvre as early as *The Bluest Eye*. Pecola, enticed into Junior's house, encounters his black cat with fascinating blue eyes, suggesting the probability that a black person can also have blue eyes. Junior ruthlessly snatches the cat from Pecola and begins to "swing it around his head in a circle." Defying Pecola's cries for him to stop, Junior lets the cat go "in midmotion" (71), throwing it against the window; it falls dead behind the radiator, its fur singeing. In a similar geometrical gesture, "Sula picked [Chicken Little] up by his hands and swung him outward then around and around," until he slips "from her hands and sailed away out over the water," still laughing in delight (60–61). When he lands in the "closed place in the water" (61), his flight, like that of the blue-eyed cat, is aborted in death. But the height and sense of the free fall he achieves brings him to the cutting edge of the kind of freedom and transcendence Sula herself seeks.

Sula's own quest for height and power through performance occurs in Eva's third floor bedroom. Mounted *on top of* Ajax in their lovemaking, Sula "rocked there, swayed there, like a Georgia pine on its knees, high above the slipping, falling smile, high above the golden eyes and the velvet helmet of hair, rocking, swaying.... She looked down, down from what seemed an awful height at the head of the man whose lemon-yellow gabardines had been the first sexual excitement she'd known. Letting her thoughts dwell on his face in order to confine, for just a while longer, the drift of her flesh toward the high silence of orgasm" (129–30). Sula's discovery of height and freedom confirming her self-centered identity and place is only partially realized because the milk-bearing Ajax, in a gesture of sexual nurture, counters her contrived image of flight with a more realistic, attainable one of his own. When Sula experiences the human frailty of love and possessiveness that ultimately destroys her at the same time that it brings her closer to Nel, she becomes just domestic enough to make the adventuresome Ajax lose interest: "when Ajax came that evening . . . the bathroom was gleaming, the bed was made, and the table was set for two" (131–32). Ajax's compelling desire, however, is to attend an air show in Dayton. Sula has indeed met her match.

Moreover, Ajax shows how trivial, self-indulgent, and incomplete is Sula's notion of the "free fall" (120), which she felt made her different from Nel, whose imagination had been driven "underground" by her repressive mother, and from the other women of Medallion. Ajax's presence heightens Sula's self-contradictions as he effectively matches her false, showy nonconformity with his more authentic eccentricity: he is the son of a conjurer mother, and his knowledge of magic and lore surpasses Sula's allure. Here Morrison's prevailing metaphor of flight begins with a leap, or free fall, and offers a rectifying alternative to Ellison's idea of hibernation. As Sula hibernates on the upper floor at 7 Carpenter Road, not in an underground cellar, she longs for the kind of performance that would complete her discovery of self-mastery and complete control. This metaphor is hinted at in *The Bluest Eye,* sketched out and challenged by Ajax in *Sula,* and finds its fullest, if not most conclusive statement in *Song of Solomon.*

The relation between Sula and Nel ruptures when Sula interprets Nel's possessiveness of her husband, Jude, to mean that Nel is one of *them,* the conventional housewives of Medallion. Nel had earlier shared Sula's vision of "the slant of life that makes it possible to stretch [life] to its limits." Becoming the clichéd wronged wife, outraged at Jude and Sula's adultery, Nel is too quickly linked with other women in the community who had "interpreted" Sula as incarnating some kind of evil. They had measured themselves morally and socially by abiding "evil"—as Pauline Breedlove did with Cholly in *The Bluest Eye*—and garnering a false dignity, even heroism, by tolerating it: "The purpose of evil was to survive it" (90). When Nel shows her natural jealousy and hurt, she begins to belong, in Sula's view, "to the town and all of its ways" (120). Nel also begins to oppose Sula's notion of invention and free fall on which Sula had based her ascendant self-mastery and their complementary friendship: "But the free fall, oh no, that required—demanded—invention: a thing to do with the wings, a way of holding the legs and most of all a full surrender to the downward flight if they wished to taste their tongues or stay alive. But alive was what they, and now Nel, did not want to be. Too dangerous" (120).

"Dangerous" more than evil is an accurate description of Sula. As an "artist with no art form" (121) Sula is vulnerable to the shifting interpretations of the only form she carries in her very being: her birthmark. Like Hannah, Sula's art lay in lovemaking, in her enjoyment of the sheer abandon of sex. This clearly is how Sula makes the leap from sexual conventions that lead to marriage and braves the outer limits of promiscuity, the ultimate breach of which is to have sex with white men. It was through carefree sex, nonetheless, that Sula found the cutting edge and the leap of free fall, her performance:

> During the lovemaking she found and needed to find the cutting edge. When she left off cooperating with her body and began to assert herself in

the act, particles of strength gathered in her like steel shavings drawn to a spacious magnetic center, forming a tight cluster that nothing, it seemed, could break. And there was utmost irony and outrage in lying *under* someone, in a position of surrender, feeling her own abiding strength and limitless power. But the cluster did break, fall apart, and in her panic to hold it together she *leaped* from the edge into soundlessness and went down howling, howling in a stinging awareness of the endings of things: an eye of sorrow in the midst of all that hurricane rage of joy. There, in the center of that silence was not eternity but the death of time and a loneliness so profound the word itself had no meaning. (122–23, emphasis mine)

In an interview published in *Nimrod,* Morrison once discussed the importance of venturing to the cutting edge and experiencing the leap. What is needed, she said, is complete self-control, divesting oneself of the vanities that weigh people down. This surrender is a triumph and results in a stark change of territory: from land to sky, from the confining boundaries of conventional morality and selfishness to the thrill of self-creation, a riding of the air. "Suppose it were literally so, what would it take to fly?" Morrison speculated. "But suppose you could just move one step up and fly? What would you have to be, and feel, and know, and do, in order to do that?" *Sula* begins to answer Morrison's own question. The author, however, asks for more: "You would have to be able to surrender, give up all of the weights, all of the vanities, all of the ignorances. And you'd have to trust and have faith in the harmony of your body. You would also have to have perfect control" (49). Sula indeed wishes for power, control, and the reward of flight. Ajax, the aviation-dreaming lover, brings her milk in blue, sky-colored glass bottles: "Ajax looked at her through the blue glass and held the milk aloft like a trophy" (127). Perhaps it is Ajax who can lift Sula from the ground, or perhaps she will lift him up into the flight and transcendence he also seeks. The only uncertainty is Sula's ability to let herself go and to release Ajax from the confining domesticity of housebound sex.

Sula fails. Her wish for total freedom, for flight, becomes as much a delusion as Pecola's blue eyes. Even the unobstructed mobility or license granted by Sula's land/birthmark is illusory because Sula is both ostracized and nourished by the same community, the same land; her mobility is limited by the interpretative needs of the community, shown by Medallion's quick regression into antagonistic behavior once the "threat" of Sula passes with her death and just prior to the parade into the tunnel. The illusory nature of Sula's desire is revealed in the contrast between her and Ajax, who, like Bigger Thomas in *Native Son* or Buster and Riley in Ellison's story "That I Had The Wings," yearns for freedom through aviation. Although Ajax's dream is realized only in his frequent trips to airports, he establishes a degree of realism against Sula's illusion of control and flight through sex. (It is he who requests that she mount him.) He thinks equally about his conjurer mother and airplanes: "when he was not sitting enchanted listening to his mother's words, he thought of airplanes, and pilots, and the deep sky that held them both" (126). The blue bottle of milk offered to Sula as a trophy connects her to the blue sky and the maternal milk. Flight and aviation as the exercise of creativity, the fulfillment of perfect control, hold both Sula and Ajax in its cobalt blue glow.

Yet the moment that Sula falls in love with Ajax and discovers possessiveness, both she and Ajax are more grounded than either desires. Ajax escapes this confinement by losing interest in Sula, but she remains trapped, totally overwhelmed by feeling human and vulnerable. When she takes Ajax through her newly cleaned house—"the spotless bathroom where dust had been swept from underneath the claw-foot tub"—she shows him her nest, a space for her hibernation, nurture, and fulfillment of sexual desire. Ajax makes love to her in the more conventional position, but he thinks less about Sula than "the date of the air show in Dayton" (134). Sula is "under" him now, and he moves "with the steadiness and the intensity of a man about to leave for Dayton" (134).

In his stunning absence, Sula tries to come to terms with her love for Ajax, for the flight of fancy he represented, for the adventuresome love, not the self-gratifying control that grounds her. Like Pecola, Sula is weighed down by the human, emotional vulnerability she succumbs to, particularly the self-willed grief she hibernates in, shut away in Eva's room. Like Cholly Breedlove, Sula reaches a momentary height of self-awareness in her admission of loneliness and possessiveness of Ajax (particularly when she realizes she never really possessed him, for she never knew his name), but she fails to give full voice to this spark of self-recognition. Hence, her freedom is never fully realized. Her flight is not only aborted, but Sula also dies. The song she wanted to sing might have saved her by providing a different kind of performance and presentation of self, as Milkman's song performance will. But the right lyrics elude her; she can only mouth repeated nonsense words. Sula, then, like Cholly, is a failed "person"-of-words, left dreaming, like Pecola, of "cobalt blue" (137) without even an air show in Dayton to claim her: "When she awoke, there was a melody in her head she could not identify or recall ever hearing before. . . . Then it came to her—the name of the song and all its lyrics just as she had heard it many times before. . . . She lay down again on the bed and sang a little wandering tune made up of the words *I have sung all the songs all the songs I have sung all the songs there are* until, touched by her own lullaby, she grew drowsy, and in the hollow of near-sleep she tasted the acridness of gold, left the chill of alabaster and smelled the dark, sweet stench of loam" (137). Sula succumbs to the "hollow," as Plum did at the "hole" of sleep, because she could not give adequate voice and action to her vision. Instead of flying, she descends to the loam of the very land that had marked her from birth.

Sula's death offers no "invention," only descent; it is neither a free fall nor the redeeming flight she had longed for. One clue to her decline lies in Morrison's verbal design of Sula's place of hibernation, Eva's room with its blind window, boarded up indirectly by Sula herself. Sula's paralyzing interest in watching her mother Hannah burn necessitated Eva's leap of rescue out of that window. When Sula subsequently dispossesses Eva of that room, she puts herself in the physical, but not the emotional, space for the reconciliation Eva had attempted in her failed rescue of Hannah, and, paradoxically, in her mercy killing of Plum—to keep him from descending further into the stupor of drugs, or reducing his already fragile maturity to the helpless state of an infant wanting a return to the womb. Instead of a womb, Eva offered Plum the scent and vision of the eagle's wings. Instead of flight, Eva's upper room offers Sula the best setting for the only perform-ance she is then capable of; her foetal plunge down an imaginary birth canal or tunnel (prefiguring the town's later disaster) is a perversion of the rebirth in death that Eva had granted Plum: "The sealed window soothed her with its sturdy termination, its unassailable finality. . . . It would be here, only here, held by this blind window high above the elm tree, that she might draw her legs up to her chest, close her eyes, put her thumb in her mouth and float over and down the tunnels, just missing the dark walls, down, down until she met a rain scent and would know the water was near, and she would curl into its heavy softness and it would envelop her, carry her, and wash her tired flesh always. Always" (148–49).

Sula's plunge into the tunnel following a period of willful hibernation completes the solitude she had always wanted. This hibernation, however, had rendered her immobile, incapacitated (except in death), for Ajax's departure and Sula's recognition of her human vulnerability stun her into physical and emotional paralysis. This backfire, or boomerang, reverses the moment of moral strength Eva felt in her husband BoyBoy's desertion, and now Eva, as a discerning, combative ancestor, cannot help Sula, for Eva has been safely locked away.

Neither Sula's solitude nor tunnel plunge is a fate left to her alone. Being a product of the land, a mark of the community, she reflects the fate of others. In the collapse of the half-finished tunnel at New River Road to the clanging tune of Sula's brother in marginality, Shadrack's pied-piper parade, the town, which had made Sula both person and pariah and a source of their negatively realized pride, meets its end. Both Sula and Shadrack have presided over figurations of the land that reveal underground refuge or hibernation to be the simple burial it is, which is what Wright's Fred Daniels discovered. Hibernation, despite the subversive bravura of Ellison's invisible man, does not lead to the effective overt activity or self-assertion he had promised. Morrison's more complex rendering of place and person in the collapse of the tunnel and the spirals of grief that bind Nel to repetitions of guilt, necessitates an end to hibernation, whether underground or three floors up. In *Song of Solomon,* Morrison offers the corrective reach of the mountaintop and a triumphant surrender to the air.

Song of Solomon. "You see?" the farm said to them. "See? See what you can do?"

Whereas the framing images in *Sula* are terrestrial enclosures, those in *Song of Solomon* are celestial flights. The novel opens with Robert Smith's aborted takeoff that brings about his planned suicide, and it ends with the violent reunion between Milkman and Guitar as one of them leaps from the mountain and into the "killing" arms of the other. The difference between the flights, how their angles of ascent exceed or grasp the long-sought-for family treasure, the home and name initially giving these characters wings, is the novel's main concern.

The novel encompasses three principal organizing structures that enlarge the orbit of cultural performances suggested thus far by several key texts, including Morrison's earlier fiction. These organizational structures include the relationship between Milkman and Guitar as the problematic moral center of the novel, the conflict between family and property ties that fuels tension between Pilate and her brother Macon Dead, and finally Milkman's initiatory "errand" into and out of the wilderness. By discovering his name and performing the song that redeems him and helps him to fly, Milkman completes the unrealized gestures and dreams of Morrison's earlier characters: Pecola, Cholly, Sula, and Ajax. *Song of Solomon* is Morrison's carefully drawn map of ancestral landscape that reclaims and resurrects moribund (the family name is Dead) or hibernating personalities.

Robert Smith, insurance salesman by day and by night a member of the "underground" radical group, the Seven Days, occupies enemy territory when he climbs to the roof of No Mercy Hospital, so called because it had never admitted black patients. Smith appears to act out the words of one Negro spiritual that describes the kind of release he desires:

> Some o' dese mornin's bright an' fair,
> Way in de middle of de air
> Goin' hitch on my wings an' try de air
> Way in de middle of de air.

Both the foreign, outer terrain of the hospital roof and the artifice involved in the "hitching" on of wings—"his wide blue silk wings curved forward around his chest" (5)—are ominous. Instead of a smooth and graceful death, Smith loses his balance, reaches for a triangle of wood jutting from the hospital's cupola, and goes "splat" (as one observer described the scene). Robert Smith's "leap" is an undignified, clumsy fall.

Smith's death sends another witness, the pregnant Ruth Foster Dead, into labor. Her son Milkman, the "little bird," whose hour of birth was accurately predicted by his aunt Pilate, who had earlier helped in his conception, becomes the first black child to be born in No Mercy. Milkman now has a more legitimate claim to the space Robert Smith had usurped. As a real "bird," a descendant of the Byrds in Shalimar, Virginia, revealed in the ending, Milkman will not need the artifice of Robert Smith's "blue silk," Ajax's cobalt blue bottles, or Pecola's "blue" eyes. Milkman's maturation in his midwestern hometown and his departure South to discover the land of his ancestors and to sing the song of Solomon—the core subject of the novel—teach him to use his own wings. Milkman's *leap* at the novel's close is a redeeming *flight.* His journey is not an easy one; nor is the novel's moral center in the magnetic friendship between Milkman and Guitar without a healthy dose of ambiguity and role reversal. Before Pilate takes over as Milkman's veritable pilot, his first navigator through a difficult childhood and adolescence is Guitar, who as a child had also witnessed

Robert Smith's fall. Guitar is best suited to be the kind of friend and adversary who can enlarge the reach of Milkman's leap "way in de middle of de air."

Guitar and Milkman do not have the same complementary personalities that make Sula and Nel appear to be one character. Although from different backgrounds, they manage to build a friendship upon mutual interests and a pendular sway of dominant and submissive roles between them as Guitar then Milkman then Guitar takes the upper hand. Older than Milkman, Guitar has the lead at first; he introduces Milkman to Pilate, whose folk conjure aided his conception and birth. Her conjure of a successful aphrodisiac had encouraged Macon and Ruth to conceive after many years of uninterest and celibacy. Pilate, who helped make Milkman's "egg," later teaches Milkman and Guitar how to make the perfect three-minute soft-boiled egg. The recipe indirectly reveals the ambiguity of love and power in their friendship and how a growing estrangement between them will be reconciled, even if in battle. "Now, the water and the egg," Pilate instructs the boys, "have to meet each other on a kind of equal standing. One can't get the upper hand over the other. So the temperature has to be the same for both" (39). In the folk logic of this equation, Milkman is the egg. What about the water? Guitar's last name is Bains, which in French means "bath" or "watering place" or both. Pilate's foolproof recipe thus becomes a formula for reconciliation; Guitar and Milkman need equal matching for either of them to assume the "perfect" control of the leap, which is the only way, as shown in *Sula,* the free fall becomes flight.

Throughout most of the novel, however, Guitar does have the upper hand. In addition to introducing Milkman to Pilate, Guitar is the one who initially guides Milkman away from his stifling, bourgeois upbringing—summers at St. Honoré Island, collecting rents for his slumlord father—and Guitar teaches Milkman the novel's core lesson: "Wanna fly, you got to give up the shit that weighs you down" (179). Until Guitar's participation in the Seven Days weakens him morally and psychologically (as had happened to mild-mannered Robert Smith) to the point where he assumes the "greed for gold" that Milkman has outgrown, Guitar, as his name suggests, is as instrumental in Milkman's development of character and cultural awareness as McKay's Banjo was for the aspiring writer Ray. That is, until Milkman finds his own voice.

The attraction of opposite social classes that initially brings Milkman and Guitar together is similar to the magnetism between Sula and Nel or the delicate class comforts that barely distinguish Pecola from Frieda and Claudia, yet allow the sisters to take Pecola under their wings. Morrison's characters appear to find stability in kinship ties and bonds of friendship that cut across class barriers and generational differences. Note the strong matrilinear network linking Eva-Hannah-Sula, for example, or the generational patterning among Pilate-Reba-Hagar. These sets of historical relationships anchor Sula and Pilate in a culture and family they use for support, particularly when the larger society rejects them as pariahs. Their hearths are comforting and inviting to Nel and Milkman, who are fleeing the stultifying middle-class repression that renders them marginal and homeless. Morrison's use of class differences as one element of mutual attraction suggests that economic conditions alone do not alienate lower or middle classes from a common culture. In *Song of Solomon* this idea is explored further when members of two different social classes represent the same family.

Macon and Pilate are brother and sister, separated after their father's murder; each inherits something different from him. Macon turns his father's love of the land and talent for farming into an obsessive ownership of property, reducing land and people to mere commodities. He advises his son Milkman: "Own things. And let the things you own own other things. Then you'll own yourself and other people too" (55). Pilate, just the opposite, already owns herself—the physical evidence of her self-possession and self-creation is her stomach without a navel. She interprets the one word uttered by her father's ghost, a regular visitor, as an admonition for performance: "Sing." Instead of acquiring property, Pilate creates song, transmitting the family lore unconsciously. The history and culture voiced here first draws Macon, then Milkman and Guitar into the charged orbit of Pilate's single-story house on Darling Street, "whose basement seemed to be rising from rather than settling into the ground" (27). Pilate's home thus moves us up out of the underground and to the mountaintop. The wings of her song first attract, then encourage full surrender to that upward motion, even for Macon, who listens surreptitiously:

> They were singing some melody that Pilate was leading. A phrase that the other two were taking up and building on. Her powerful contralto, Reba's piercing soprano in counterpoint, and the soft voice of the girl, Hagar, who must be about ten or eleven now, pulled him like a carpet tack under the influence of a magnet.

160

Surrendering to the sound, Macon moved closer. He wanted no conversation, no witness, only to listen and perhaps to see the three of them, the source of that music that made him think of fields and wild turkey and calico. (29)

As Macon peers unseen into the lives of these women, he becomes a version of Wright's man who lived underground or of Ellison's invisible man. Lacking Daniels's cynicism, Macon secretly yearns to come out of hibernation and to accept fully the family he had denied in his "drive for wealth" (28): "Near the window, hidden by the dark, he felt the irritability of the day drain from him and relished the effortless beauty of the women singing in the candlelight. . . . As Macon felt himself softening under the weight of memory and music, the song died down. The air was quiet and yet Macon Dead could not leave. He liked looking at them freely this way" (29-30).

Macon is the kind of invisible man Milkman refuses to be. Without ever learning all that his nickname means (the prolonged "sexual" nursing from his mother and the demands of nurture he places on other women), Milkman will develop any trait, any *device,* to differentiate himself from his father, even to the point of affecting a limp. "Milkman feared his father, respected him, but knew, because of the leg, that he could never emulate him. So he differed from him as much as he dared" (63). Unlike Macon, who listens from outside, Milkman penetrates Pilate's house and there learns the magic in the perfect meeting of egg and water.

Macon and Pilate vie for a controlling influence over Milkman. They also compete over their relation to the dead father and to the farmland that was as fertile as it was generous, "See? See what you can do?" The father had made it the best farming in Montour County, earning him the adoration of blacks and the enmity of the whites who eventually killed him. The land and the family heritage become battlegrounds for the continuing struggle between Pilate and Macon. While Macon is an owner of land and of people (his assistant Sonny, his tenant Porter), or so he thinks, Pilate, like Cholly Breedlove, is a "renting" black. Their different relation to the land inversely determines how they function in the novel to help or hinder Milkman. Macon remains dead to the past, which is celebrated and *possessed* unself-consciously by Pilate. Macon, defeated by his father's murder, has leased his identity to fluctuations in the real estate market and in the whims of bank lenders out of desperation to prove his worth. Pilate, on the other hand, a restless wanderer, owns only those objects that implicitly direct her search for place (and for refuge from pariah status): rocks, a sack of human bones, and a geography book—her only legacy until she nurtures Milkman. Instead of washing her hands free of the past, she fills them with such common objects, burdens really, until Milkman's discovery shows them to be the family treasure they always were. By identifying the invisible ancestor in Pilate's song—"reading and re-reading" Pilate's oral poetry—Milkman lifts the burden of those bones from Pilate's shoulders and allows her to experience a surrender to the air that prefigures his more complete flight.

Cursed with endless wandering because the lack of a navel relegates her to pariah status in whatever community she finds herself, Pilate and her smooth stomach, like Sula and her birthmark, are objects of interpretation. Unlike Sula's artistic formlessness, Pilate has her bootlegging business, her conjure, and most importantly, her song—the same song that announced Robert Smith's presence on the hospital roof and that cushioned his awkward, suicidal descent; the same song that drew Macon to her part of town and partially out of his preferred invisibility. It is also the song neither Sula nor Cholly could sing. Like the Negro spiritual encoding messages for escape or resistance, it contains the riddle and the answer to the question of survival; it is a mystery to be unraveled, like the enigmatic advice of the grandfather in *Invisible Man.* This is the poem Milkman will hear again and again until he recites it by heart; his performance in the land of his ancestors reveals the hidden family name:

> O *Sugarman done fly away*
> *Sugarman done gone*
> *Sugarman cut across the sky*
> *Sugarman gone home. . . . (6)*

When Milkman learns the full text of the song and the history transmitted through it—"Jake the only son of Solomon"—he recognizes the ancestor and the homeland Pilate perhaps had been reading about in her frayed geography book. She can now let go of the burden of bones. She buries them and her earring locket, containing her name written by her father, in a mountaintop grave. The interment of the bones also signals Pilate's end, for she is killed by a bullet intended for Milkman. Once again, she gives him life, if only for the time it takes Guitar to exchange his gun for his fists. More important, however, Pilate's death concludes her terrestrial wandering. When a bird, attracted by the glittering earring near her crumpled body, swoops down and soars away with the locket, Pilate achieves symbolic flight. She experiences the full meaning of her ancestry among the Flying Africans and of her name, no longer Pilate but *pilot* (a fulfillment that eludes LeRoi Jones's Air Force gunner and Ellison's flight trainee). The meaning of the novel's epigraph also comes clear: *"The fathers may soar / And the children may know their names."* In addition to wholeness of identity, Pilate achieves at last her rightful, celestial place.

Macon Dead, on the other hand, remains grounded in his lust for gold and in his accumulation of property. He has misread the lesson his father had learned from the land and its harvest, as heard in Morrison's thrilling rendition of the sermon the land itself delivers:

> "You see?" the farm said to them. "See? See what you can do?... Here, this here, is what a man can do if he puts his mind to it and his back in it. Stop sniveling," it said. "Stop picking around the edges of the world. Take advantage, and if you can't take advantage, take disadvantage. We live here. On this planet, in this nation, in this country right here. *No* where else! We got a home in this rock, don't you see! Nobody starving in my home; nobody crying in my home, and if I got a home you got one too! Grab it. Grab this land! Take it, hold it, my brothers, make it, my brothers, shake it, squeeze it, turn it, twist it, beat it, kick it, kiss it, whip it, stomp it ... own it, build it, multiply it, and pass it on—can you hear me? Pass it on!" (235)

This land, its voice full of the language and cadence of Negro spirituals and rich with sources of identity, should offer prosperity to any family willing to use it in the ways suggested above, not merely acquire more and more of it. The land is to be used for procreation and harvest, not hibernation and greed. Thus, in many respects, Macon remains invisible to the land, to the community, to his family, and finally, to the culture that commands him to perform, not just to listen secretively. In the conflict between Macon and Pilate over the land, over history, and over Milkman, Pilate wins because she has shown Milkman a way out of the hibernation advocated by Macon's inertia. In this way, too, Milkman's struggle enlarges the orbit of geography for Afro-American identity and cultural performance beyond the cave of hibernation promoted in Ellison's *Invisible Man*.

Song of Solomon signals a major break from Ellison's territoriality in Afro-American letters, yet Morrison's thematic and imagistic challenge to

Ellison begins with interesting points of comparison to his novel. These common areas of concern suggest Morrison's careful reading of Ellison and the detour she takes from his "highway," and from the theme, setting, language, and literary form he enshrined. Morrison's break becomes all the more bold, startling, and significant because the comparisons suggest that she has explored Ellison's terrain and found it lacking in the kind of cultural mobility her characters and their experiences demand.

Morrison completes the groping for avian imagery and the search for redemptive flight first articulated in slave songs and narratives and then imagined more existentially in texts by Wright, Ellison, and LeRoi Jones. Morrison's aviators, the Air Force men who frequent a local bar, inspire Milkman's envy only until he discovers that he can fly without the encumbrance of military obligations. She also manipulates and enlarges the conventions of surrealism and the *bildungsroman,* which Ellison viewed as granting the writer freedom from the sociological predilections and realistic persuasions most readers impose upon black American fiction. This was Ellison's main criticism of Wright, but his injunction stops there. Morrison undercuts the hegemony of Ellison's preferred narrative strategy, what Robert Stepto has called "the narrative of hibernation" (193), by enlarging the structure to encompass multiple lives and points of view as her characters aim for motion, not stasis. The multiplicity of perspectives and situations in Morrison's fiction requires protagonists writ large; her novels are *bildungsromans* of entire communities and racial idioms rather than the voice of a single individual. What central protagonist exists develops only through the interplay between the community and the individual. Even Milkman is admonished by his father to "know the whole story" before taking sides. "And if you want to be a whole man, you have to deal with the whole truth" (70). Morrison's novels require us to read the life of a community as the text and context of an individual's articulation of voice. Milkman needs the play of the children of Shalimar to help him hear Jake's "narrative" in the song and to "close" the story of his own self-possession. Milkman's cultural performance when he sings the song of Solomon makes him a successful man-of-words.

Other parallels are at work and play between Morrison and Ellison. Both their protagonists struggle against an identity imposed by others. The nameless invisible man must end his passivity and willingness to be named by others, from the letters sent by Bledsoe to the slip of paper revealing the Brotherhood's name for him. Morrison's protagonist must come to terms with a nickname whose origin he never knows and with people who want to "use" him: "Somehow everybody was using him for something or as something. Working out some scheme of their own on him, making him the subject of their dreams of wealth, or love, or martyrdom" (165). Sonny, when he discovers Ruth's prolonged nursing of her son, announces, "A natural milkman if ever I seen one. Look out womens. Here he come" (15). Milkman feels his name to be "dirty, intimate, and hot" (15) as he grows up to fulfill, unwittingly, Sonny's double-edged prophecy: he will take from women, but he will also be a passive, bleached, colorless (invisible?) personality until he takes charge of himself, shares himself with others. When Milkman learns through his journey to the South that names can bear witness, indeed "had meaning," he can give up his old self more easily (he loses his fine clothes and jewelry and car while on his journey) and reciprocate in lovemaking with Sweet more than he had done with any other woman ("He washed her hair. . . . He made up the bed. . . . He washed the dishes. . . . She kissed his mouth. He touched her face. She said please come back. He said I'll see you tonight" [285]). Milkman's increased awareness of the mutual responsibilities in love and self-discovery brings about his visibility.

Both novels also share a figuration of geography that shapes the protagonists' journeys. Ellison's narrative (apart from the frame) moves from the South to the North; Morrison moves from the North to the South. She alters the direction of cultural history away from simple chronology and toward a single, charged moment of multiple discoveries by emphasizing Milkman's embrace of cultural and familial geography. He arrives at the ancestral ground to become rooted in it as deep and as high as Pilate's father's bones. The protagonists in both novels also confront a riddle that invites interpretation and subversion of the nameless condition of Afro-Americans: one proffered by Ellison's protagonist's grandfather, the other by Morrison's "Sugarman" or Milkman's great-great-great grandfather, whose identity could save his life. Both narratives or novels are framed or enclosed; one by the static posture of *telling* a story through the device of prologue and epilogue, the other by dual *actions* that are dynamic performances: Smith's suicide is revised in Milkman's flight.

Although Ellison's protagonist's writing of *Invisible Man* in his underground retreat can be seen as an active deed (since it creates the space and action of the novel), Morrison offers an effective contrast: She replaces the cellar-basement environment for the invisible man's *written* performance with the mountaintop height of Milkman's *oral* performance. Also significant is their different treatment of flight. Ellison offers the folk rhyme "They picked poor robin clean" as a warning about the protagonist's grounded predicament. Morrison counteracts with the myth of the Flying Africans to show Milkman the reach and promise of the air, *if* he can ride it. Milkman becomes a true descendant of Jake, the only son of Solomon, whereas Ellison's protagonist fails to become a true blood following Trueblood's example of storytelling and rhetorical flourish. When Milkman actually sings the song of Solomon, he assumes the name that had been denied the invisible man, without which Milkman would be colorless and the land of his culture invisible to all. Milkman can now nurture others: Pilate, Ruth, Sweet, Jake, and himself. From that exchange of emotional commitment, Milkman gains the strength he needs to meet his adversary Guitar and gain an equal if not *upper* hand.

Above and beyond these various points of comparison between *Song of Solomon* and *Invisible Man* lies Morrison's most significant achievement. She extends the geographical imagery and enriches the acts of deliverance established so far in Afro-American letters. Her novel encompasses the three principal landscapes of retreat and regeneration already present in black American culture: the wilderness, the underground, and the mountaintop. Taken as part of Morrison's assessment of geography and identity in fiction, they exceed earlier attempts to fix or promote one region over another. *Song of Solomon* not only returns us to landscapes suggested in the slave songs and narratives, it also plays upon the fundamental contrast between underground and mountain stages of self-achievement, thus exposing the limits of a Wright-Ellison geography and moving us forward to other heights of self-awareness through action.

Macon and Pilate Dead, for all their successes and failures, are still connected to figures of spatial enclosures, even the imminent grave suggested by their unfortunate family name. They are also prisoners of a haunting guilt in having killed a miner at the mouth of a cave in the wilderness through which they wandered aimlessly after their father's death. Once overcoming the menacing miner—a digger of undergrounds probing for hidden treasures below—the two children are prepared to conquer other spaces, such as houses, later on. Pilate's single-story dwelling appears to rise from the basement or underground, and Macon's acquisition of property represents his rise in society. Yet both are still tied to either material goods or to the alternative meaning they can convey, which is how Fred Daniels reacted to the bank notes and diamonds in his cave. It is Milkman who eventually develops a more effective relation to the land when he confronts the wilderness. There he not only searches for the cave where the miner's gold is presumably hidden, but he is prepared for the strenuous encounter with the Shalimar woods during the nighttime hunt of the bobcat with Calvin and King Walker and the other men of the town. They hate him at first ("They looked with hatred at the city Negro who could buy a car as if it were a bottle of whiskey because the one he had was broken" [266]), but Milkman's participation in the hunt gains their fraternity and friendship. He secures his own place in the ancestral territory apart from the claims of Pilate or Macon.

It is not enough, however, for Milkman simply to arrive in Shalimar, or to lose his material possessions while there (the vanities that weigh him down). He has to walk that lonesome valley, as the slave songs required, by himself:

> There was nothing here to help him—not his money, his car, his father's reputation, his suit, or his shoes. In fact, they hampered him. Except for his broken watch, and his wallet with about two hundred dollars, all he had started out with on his journey was gone. . . . His watch and his two hundred dollars would be of no help out here, where all a man had was what he was born with, or had learned to use. And endurance. Eyes, ears, nose, taste, touch—and some other sense that he knew he did not have: an ability to separate out, of all the things there were to sense, the one that life itself might depend on. (277)

Milkman has to earn kinship by enduring the woods, the wilderness. Like the fugitive in slave narratives, he has to renew his covenant with nature to secure passage out of the wilderness that had invited him in. Only through this initiatory trial in the woods of Blue Ridge County will he encounter those figures of the landscape that will give definite meaning to the otherwise confusing names and places in the children's song:

> *Jay the only son of Solomon*
> *Come booba yale, come booba tambee*
> *Whirl about and touch the sun*
> *Come booba yalle, come booba tambee . . .* (264)

Each step of his way puts Milkman "on land that sloped upward" (274). Only by surviving the wilderness—which is not a foregone conclusion since he is caught off-guard by the now crazed, nightseeing, cat-eyed Guitar, who,

167

with this unfair advantage, cannot "kill" Milkman yet because the water and egg need equal matching—does Milkman learn the historical meaning associated with two figures of landscape that lie beyond the vision and experience of Macon or Pilate: Ryna's Gulch and Solomon's Leap, a valley and a mountaintop. These contrasting, gender-related spaces extend from Morrison's earlier survey of cultural territory used as the framing images in *Sula:* the hilltop Bottom leading to the collapsing tunnel. Here the movement is reversed. Ryna's Gulch (as well as the bodies of the women Milkman has exploited through sexual conquest) points him to Solomon's Leap, but only after Milkman has bent his ear to the ground to hear the land's sermon or "anything the earth had to say" (279). Milkman's discovery of these new spaces and new territories, makes him the pilot to guide Pilate to the resting place for her father's bones.

In this wilderness, Milkman earns friendship with the men of Shalimar, with himself, and with the earth. Milkman discovers that he can be his own man, based on his proven skills of survival. Walking on the earth like he belonged to it, Milkman no longer needs the artificial device, the dutchman, of his limp to distinguish himself from his father. Nor does he need material possessions to differentiate himself from the kinsmen of Shalimar. Sharing at last a good-hearted laugh with them, Milkman becomes exhilarated "by simply walking the earth. Walking it like he belonged on it; like his legs were stalks, tree trunks, a part of his body that extended down down down into the rock and soil, and were comfortable there—on the earth and on the place where he walked. And he did not limp" (281). Here Milkman becomes rooted. "Back home he had never felt that way, as though he belonged to anyplace or anybody" (293). This belonging enables him to decode the children's rhyme that gives meaning to the landscape and to Milkman's ancestry. Caught without pencil or paper, Milkman cannot write the song down, as Ellison's protagonist could do with his narrative. Milkman "would just have to listen and memorize it" (303), internalize it.

When Milkman leads Pilate to Shalimar, he brings her similar homelessness to an end: she "blended into the population like a stick of butter in a churn" (335). Together they advance to the higher ground of Solomon's Leap, both to bury the bones and to meet their separate fates. Pilate will fly without ever leaving the ground, comforted by Milkman's rendition of the song, which Morrison leaves unindented and without italics on the page to suggest that it has been refashioned in Milkman's voice and fused into the uninterrupted flow of the narrative: "Sugargirl don't leave me here / Cotton balls to choke me / Sugargirl don't leave me here / Buckra's arms to yoke me" (336). Now Milkman can ride the air. His leap of surrender is his ultimate performance, a flight he has earned by doffing his vanities and passing the test of the wilderness. His leap transcends the rootedness and the freedom he has gained. Milkman and Morrison's flight, their ride out of the wilderness, demonstrates self-mastery and perfect control.

Bibliography

Abrahams, Roger D. *The Man-of-Words in the West Indies: Performance and the Emergence of Creole Culture.* Baltimore: Johns Hopkins University Press, 1983.

Allen, William Francis, Charles Pickard Ware, and Lucy McKim Garrison. *Slave Songs of the United States.* New York: Peter Smith, 1867.

Baker, Houston A., Jr. *Singers of Daybreak: Studies in Black American Literature.* Washington, D.C.: Howard University Press, 1974.

Baldwin, James. *The Amen Corner.* New York: Dial, 1968.

———. *Another Country.* New York: Dial, 1962.

———. *The Fire Next Time.* New York: Dial, 1963.

———. *Giovanni's Room.* New York: Dial, 1956.

———. *Go Tell It on the Mountain.* New York: Dial, 1953.

———. *If Beale Street Could Talk.* New York: Dial, 1974.

———. "James Baldwin Back Home." Interview by Robert Coles. *The New York Times Book Review,* 31 July 1977.

———. *Just Above My Head.* New York: Dial, 1979.

———. *No Name in the Street.* New York: Dial, 1972.

———. *Nobody Knows My Name: More Notes of a Native Son.* New York: Dial, 1961.

———. "Sonny's Blues." In *Going to Meet the Man,* 101–41. New York: Dial, 1965.

Bauman, Richard. *Verbal Art as Performance.* Rowly, Mass.: Newbury House, 1977.

Bibb, Henry. "Narrative of the Life and Adventures of Henry Bibb, an American Slave." 1849. Reprinted in *Puttin' On Ole Massa,* edited by Gilbert Osofsky, 51–171. New York: Harper, 1969.

Blassingame, John. *The Slave Community.* New York: Oxford University Press, 1972.

———, ed. *Slave Testimony: Two Centuries of Letters, Speeches, Interviews and Autobiographies.* Baton Rouge: Louisiana State University Press, 1977.

Bloom, Harold. *The Anxiety of Influence: A Theory of Poetry.* New York: Oxford University Press, 1973.

Brent, Linda. *Incidents in the Life of a Slave Girl.* 1861. Reprint. New York: Harvest-Harcourt, 1973.

Brown, Henry "Box." "Shipped to Freedom." In *Black Men in Chains: Narratives by Escaped Slaves,* edited by Charles H. Nichols, 179-99. New York: Lawrence Hill, 1972.

Brown, William Wells. "Narrative of William Wells Brown, a Fugitive Slave." 1847. Reprinted in *Puttin' On Ole Massa,* edited by Gilbert Osofsky, 173-223. New York: Harper, 1969.

Davis, Charles T. *Black Is the Color of the Cosmos: Essays on Afro-American Literature and Culture, 1941-1981.* Edited by Henry Louis Gates, Jr. New York: Garland, 1982.

Dixon, Melvin. "O Mary Rambo Don't You Weep." *The Carleton Miscellany* 18 (Winter 1980): 98-104.

Douglass, Frederick. *The Life and Times of Frederick Douglass.* 1881. Reprint. New York: Bonanza, 1962.

——. *Narrative of the Life of Frederick Douglass, an American Slave, Written by Himself.* 1845. Reprint. Cambridge, Mass.: Belknap Press of Harvard University Press, 1960.

Du Bois, William E. B. Review of *Banjo,* by Claude McKay. *The Crisis* (July 1929).

——. *The Souls of Black Folk.* Chicago: A. C. McClurg, 1903.

Ellison, Ralph. "Flying Home." In *Cross Section,* edited by Edwin Seaver, 469-85. New York: L. B. Fischer, 1944. Reprinted in *The Best Short Stories by Negro Writers,* edited by Langston Hughes, 151-70. Boston: Little Brown, 1967.

——. *Invisible Man.* Thirtieth Anniversary Edition. New York: Random House, 1982.

——. *Shadow and Act.* New York: Random House, 1953.

Fabre, Genevieve. *Drumbeats, Masks, and Metaphor: Contemporary Afro-American Theater.* Translated by Melvin Dixon. Cambridge: Harvard University Press, 1983.

Fabre, Michel. "Richard Wright: The Man Who Lived Underground." *Studies in the Novel* 3 (1971):165-79.

Genovese, Eugene. *Roll, Jordan, Roll: The World The Slaves Made.* New York: Pantheon, 1974.

Harper, Michael S., and Robert B. Stepto, eds. *Chant of Saints: A Gathering of Afro-American Literature, Art, and Scholarship.* Urbana: University of Illinois Press, 1979.

Henson, Josiah. *Father Henson's Story of His Own Life.* 1858. Reprint. New York: Corinth Books, 1962.

Hughes, Langston. "The Negro Artist and the Racial Mountain." *The Nation* 122 (1926):692-94.

Hurston, Zora Neale. *Dust Tracks on a Road.* 1942. Edited by Robert E. Hemenway. 2d ed. Urbana: University of Illinois Press, 1984.

———. *Spunk: The Selected Stories of Zora Neale Hurston.* Berkeley: Turtle Island Foundation, 1985.

———. *Their Eyes Were Watching God.* 1937. Reprint. Urbana: University of Illinois Press, 1978.

Johnson, James Weldon. *The Autobiography of an Ex-Coloured Man.* 1912. Reprint. New York: Hill and Wang, 1960.

———. Preface to *The Book of American Negro Poetry.* New York: Harcourt, 1958.

———, and J. Rosamond Johnson. *The Book of American Negro Spirituals.* New York: Viking, 1925.

Jones, Gayl. *Corregidora.* New York: Random House, 1975.

———. "Deep Song." In *Chant of Saints: A Gathering of Afro-American Literature, Art, and Scholarship,* edited by Michael S. Harper and Robert B. Stepto, 376. Urbana: University of Illinois Press, 1979.

———. *Eva's Man.* New York: Random House, 1976.

———. Interview by Michael S. Harper. In *Chant of Saints: A Gathering of Afro-American Literature, Art, and Scholarship,* edited by Michael S. Harper and Robert B. Stepto, 352-75. Urbana: University of Illinois Press, 1979.

Jones, LeRoi. *The Dead Lecturer.* New York: Grove, 1964.

———. *Dutchman and The Slave.* New York: William Morrow, 1964.

———. *The System of Dante's Hell.* New York: Grove, 1965.

Jones, Thomas. *The Experience of Thomas H. Jones.* Boston: Bazin and Chandler, 1862.

Levine, Lawrence W. "Slave Songs and Slave Consciousness." In *American Negro Slavery,* edited by Allen Weinstein and Frank Otto Gatell, 153-82. 2d ed. New York: Oxford University Press, 1973.

Lewis, David L. *King: A Critical Biography.* New York: Praeger, 1970.

Marx, Leo. *The Machine in the Garden: Technology and the Pastoral Ideal in America.* New York: Oxford University Press, 1964.

Mays, Benjamin. *The Negro's God as Reflected in his Literature.* New York: Atheneum, 1968.

McKay, Claude. *Banana Bottom.* 1933. Reprint. New York: Harvest-Harcourt, 1961.

———. *Banjo: A Story without a Plot.* 1929. Reprint. New York: Harvest-Harcourt, 1957.

———. *Home to Harlem.* 1928. Reprint. Chatham, N.J.: The Chatham Bookseller, 1973.

———. *A Long Way From Home.* 1937. Reprint. New York: Arno Press and The New York Times, 1969.

———. *Selected Poems of Claude McKay.* New York: Bookman Associates, 1953.

———. "To Max Eastman." Letter, 3 December 1934. In *The Passion of Claude McKay: Selected Poetry and Prose, 1912–1948,* edited by Wayne Cooper. New York: Schocken, 1973.

Morrison, Toni. *The Bluest Eye.* New York: Holt, 1970.

———. Interview by Pepsi Charles. *Nimrod* 21 and 22 (1977):43–51.

———. " 'Intimate Things in Place': A Conversation with Toni Morrison." Interview by Robert B. Stepto. In *Chant of Saints: A Gathering of Afro-American Literature, Art, and Scholarship,* edited by Michael S. Harper and Robert B. Stepto, 213–29. Urbana: University of Illinois Press, 1979.

———. *Song of Solomon.* New York: Knopf, 1977.

———. *Sula.* New York: Knopf, 1974.

———. *Tar Baby.* New York: Knopf, 1981.

Murray, Albert. *The Hero and the Blues.* Columbia: University of Missouri Press, 1973.

Nash, Roderick. *Wilderness and the American Mind.* Rev. ed. New Haven: Yale University Press, 1973.

Nichols, Charles H. *Many Thousand Gone: The Ex-Slaves Account of Their Bondage and Freedom.* 1963. Reprint. Bloomington: Indiana University Press, 1969.

Parker, William. "Fugitives Resist Kidnapping." In *Black Men in Chains: Narratives by Escaped Slaves,* edited by Charles H. Nichols, 280–315. New York: Lawrence Hill, 1972.

Ramchand, Kenneth. *The West Indian Novel and Its Background.* London: Faber, 1970.

Redding, J. Saunders. *To Make a Poet Black.* 1939. Reprint. College Park, Md.: McGrath, 1968.

Seaver, Edwin, ed. *Cross Section.* New York: L. B. Fischer, 1944.

Skerrett, Joseph T., Jr. "Take My Burden Up: Three Studies in Psychobiographical Criticism and Afro-American Fiction." Ph.D. diss., Yale University, 1975.

Starling, Marion. "The Slave Narrative: Its Place in American Literary History." Ph.D. diss., New York University, 1946.

Stepto, Robert B. *From Behind the Veil: A Study of Afro-American Narrative.* Urbana: University of Illinois Press, 1979.

Tate, Claudia, ed. *Black Women Writers at Work.* New York: Continuum, 1983.

Thompson, John. *The Life of John Thompson.* 1856. Reprint. Westport: Negro Universities Press, 1968.

Toomer, Jean. *Cane.* New York: Boni & Liveright, 1923.

———. "To Waldo Frank." Letter, 12 December 1922. In *Black Is the Color of the Cosmos: Essays on Afro-American Literature and Culture, 1941-1981,* edited by Henry Louis Gates, Jr. New York: Garland, 1982.

———. *The Wayward and the Seeking.* Edited by Darwin T. Turner. Washington, D.C.: Howard University Press, 1980.

Turner, Darwin T. *In a Minor Chord: Three Afro-American Writers and Their Search for Identity.* Carbondale: Southern Illinois University Press, 1971.

Turner, Nat. *The Confessions of Nat Turner.* Edited by Thomas Gray. 1831. Reprinted in *Nat Turner's Slave Rebellion,* edited by Herbert Aptheker. New York: Grove, 1968.

Vassa, Gustavus. *The Interesting Narrative of Olaudah Equiano, or Gustavus Vassa, The African. Written by Himself.* 1789. Reprinted in *Great Slave Narratives,* edited by Arna Bontemps, 1-192. Boston: Beacon, 1969.

Walker, Alice. *The Color Purple.* New York: Harcourt, 1982.

———. *In Search of Our Mothers' Gardens: Womanist Prose.* San Diego: Harcourt, 1983.

———. *Meridian.* New York: Harcourt, 1976.

———. *Revolutionary Petunias and Other Poems.* New York: Harcourt, 1973.

———. *The Third Life of Grange Copeland.* New York: Harcourt, 1970.

Wright, Richard. *American Hunger.* New York: Harper, 1977.

———. "Between Laughter and Tears." Review of *Their Eyes Were Watching God,* by Zora Neale Hurston. *New Masses* (5 Oct. 1937):22-25.

———. "Between the World and Me." *Partisan Review* (2 July–August 1935): 18-19. Reprinted in *Richard Wright Reader,* edited by Ellen Wright and Michel Fabre, 246-47. New York: Harper, 1978.

———. *Black Boy: A Record of Childhood and Youth.* New York: Harper, 1945.

———. "How 'Bigger' Was Born." *Saturday Review* (June 1940):4-20. Reprinted as introduction to *Native Son,* vii-xxxiv. New York: Harper, 1940.

———. "The Man Who Lived Underground." Earlier ms. Richard Wright Archives, Beinecke Library, Yale University, New Haven, Connecticut.

———. "The Man Who Lived Underground." In *Cross Section,* edited by Edwin Seaver, 58-102. New York: L. B. Fischer, 1944. Reprinted in *Richard Wright Reader,* edited by Ellen Wright and Michel Fabre, 517-76. New York: Harper, 1978.

———. "Memories of My Grandmother." Unpublished ms. Richard Wright Archives, Beinecke Library, Yale University, New Haven, Connecticut.

———. *The Outsider.* New York: Harper, 1953.

———. *12 Million Black Voices: A Folk History of the Negro in the United States.* New York: Viking, 1941.

———. *Uncle Tom's Children.* New York: Harper, 1940.

Zahan, Dominique. *The Religion, Spirituality, and Thought of Traditional Africa.* Translated by Kate Ezra Martin and Lawrence M. Martin. Chicago: University of Chicago Press, 1979.

Index

A Note on the Author

Melvin Dixon is professor of English at Queens College, the City University of New York. He is a graduate of Wesleyan University and received his Ph.D. from Brown University. Mr. Dixon is the author of *Change of Territory* (poetry), the translator of Genevieve Fabre's *Drumbeats, Masks, and Metaphor: Contemporary Afro-American Theatre,* and the author of several articles in books such as *The Slave's Narrative: Texts and Contexts* and *Black Women Writers (1950-1980): A Critical Evaluation.*